W9-BLA-983

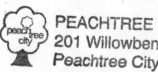

Marie Curie

Pioneer Physicist

by Carol Greene

 CHILDRENS PRESS, CHICAGO

ACKNOWLEDGMENTS

Excerpts from *Madame Curie, A Biography* by Eve Curie.
Copyright © 1937 by Doubleday & Company, Inc.
Reprinted by permission of the publisher.

PICTURE ACKNOWLEDGMENTS

Culver Pictures, Inc.—Frontispiece, pages 8, 30, 53, 54, 56, 58
The Bettmann Archive—pages 51, 59 (right), 75, 99
Historical Pictures Service, Inc., Chicago—page 55
UPI—pages 57, 59 (left), 60, 105

Cover illustration by Len W. Meents

Library of Congress Cataloging in Publication Data

Greene, Carol.
  Marie Curie, pioneer physicist.

  Includes index.
  Summary: A biography of the brilliant scientist
whose work with radioactivity caused her death, but gave
life to others.
  1. Curie, Marie, 1867-1934—Juvenile literature.
2. Chemists—Poland—Biography—Juvenile literature.
[1. Curie, Marie, 1867-1934. 2. Chemists] I. Title.
QD22.C8G74 1984   530′.092′4 [B] [92]   83-26273
ISBN 0-516-03203-8

1 2 3 4 5 6 7 8 9 10 R 93 92 91 90 89 88 87 86 85 84

DEDICATION

This book is for Jessica Medford.

Note on spelling of family names:

Women with Polish family names ending in i often change the i to an a, which is a feminine ending. For instance, women in the Sklodowski family spell their name Sklodowska; men spell theirs Sklodowski.

Table of Contents

Chapter 1

LITTLE MANYA

The small boarding school on Freta Street looked perfectly normal that day. Outside, a cold Warsaw wind howled around the corners. Dead leaves skittered along the cobblestones. But inside, the girls were warm and busy with their lessons.

In her apartment at the school, Mrs. Sklodowska was busy, too. It wasn't easy to take care of her husband and children and also act as principal of the school. But on that day, suddenly, she stopped working. Her chores would have to wait. It was time.

Soon little girls were running in and out of the apartment. Some carried sheets. Some carried pillows. But most carried jars of hot water. And there in the school on Freta Street, Marya Salomee Sklodowska was born. The date was November 7, 1867.

It wasn't an easy time to be born in Poland. The country had been carved into three pieces. Austria owned one, Germany another, and Russia the third. The Sklodowski family lived in the Russian section.

The Russians wanted the Polish people under their rule to stop being Poles. They wouldn't let them use the Polish lan-

Opposite, left to right: Manya Sklodowska (Marie Curie), her father, and her sisters Bronya and Hela in 1890

guage in schools. Everyone had to speak Russian. Polish courts were closed. The best jobs went to Russians. Spies skulked around to make sure the Poles followed the rules. Polish people who fought back were sent to Siberia—or had their heads chopped off. Even the name "Poland" was taken off the official maps. Instead the area was called "Vistula Land." (The Vistula is a river in Poland.)

But no time ever has been an easy time for the Polish people. For centuries, invaders have tried to take over that stubborn country. But the Poles have gone right on being Poles and fighting back.

Nobody called the new little Pole Marya Salomee for long. Polish people like nicknames. Soon they were calling the baby Manyusska. Or Anciupecio. But most of the time they called her Manya.

After Manya's birth, the Sklodowskis moved to an apartment in another school, a boys' high school. There Manya's father, Professor Sklodowski, taught mathematics and physics and worked as the school's underinspector.

The director of the school, a Mr. Ivanov, also had an apartment in the school building. He was one of those spies who tried to catch Polish people breaking the law. When she grew older, Manya would walk very quietly past the windows of Mr. Ivanov's apartment. She hated the man who lived behind those lace curtains. Her whole family hated him. They were afraid of him, too.

But Manya didn't spend all her time worrying about Mr. Ivanov. She was too busy growing up and having fun. It was wonderful having an older brother and three older sisters. They all loved her and spent time playing with her.

Zosia, the oldest sister, told marvelous stories. She wrote funny plays and acted them out. Manya could listen to her for hours. Since Zosia was seven years older than Manya, she helped take care of the little girl. For Manya, it was almost like having two mothers.

Joseph, the boy, was next oldest. Then came Bronya, then Hela. Manya played games with them. Sometimes they built castles and cathedrals out of blocks. They used the blocks for ammunition in war games. During summer vacations, they made mud pies, climbed trees, and picked gooseberries or cherries.

When Manya was four, she played a special game with her sister Bronya. Bronya was supposed to be learning the alphabet. She decided to play school with little Manya and teach *her* the alphabet instead. She used cardboard letters to do it.

One day Bronya and Manya were with their parents. Bronya was reading a lesson aloud. It was an easy lesson, but poor Bronya was having a hard time.

Finally Manya could stand it no longer. She took the book away from her sister. Then she began reading the lesson— perfectly.

Her mother and father just stared at her. Bronya looked a little angry. Suddenly Manya stopped reading and burst into tears.

"Pardon!" she cried. "I didn't do it on purpose. It's only because it was so easy!"

She was afraid she had done something wrong by learning how to read.

Manya wasn't often afraid of her parents. They were good, wise, gentle people, and she adored them. Her mother had been a teacher and principal for many years. After Manya was born, she had decided to stop teaching. She had enough children of her own to look after.

Mrs. Sklodowska was a musician. She could play the piano and sing. But those skills weren't much help when the family was short of money—and they always were. So she taught herself a new skill—cobbling. Before long she was making all the children's shoes. It wasn't easy work, but she never grumbled. One did what had to be done. That was a rule for Mrs. Sklodowska.

The Roman Catholic religion was very important to her, as it always has been to many Polish people. She liked to go to church every day. She would kneel for long periods of time, praying. This impressed little Manya.

But most of all, Manya liked to sit near her mother at home and watch her work or listen to her talk. Sometimes her mother would smile or touch Manya's hair. But she never kissed her. In fact, Mrs. Sklodowska never kissed or hugged any of her children.

When Manya was older, she learned the reason for her mother's strange behavior. Mrs. Sklodowska had tuberculosis, a serious disease that was also very contagious. To help protect the children from catching it, she didn't hug or kiss them. And to keep them from worrying about her, she didn't tell them what was wrong.

Manya's father worried, though. Sometimes his face looked terribly sad. But most of the time his children probably believed he was worried about money—or Mr. Ivanov.

Just the thought of Mr. Ivanov made Professor Sklodowski's children furious. Because of him, their father wasn't allowed to teach the way he wanted to. And the professor was such a smart man. He had even studied in St. Petersburg, Russia. He really loved learning—especially learning about science—and he could make it exciting for others to learn.

Professor Sklodowski wasn't a scary sort of father either, though he knew the difference between right and wrong and taught it to his children. Sometimes little Manya even crawled up into his lap to play with his tie or pull his beard.

The whole family spent a great deal of time in what they called the workroom. There Mrs. Sklodowska tapped away with her cobbler's hammer. Professor Sklodowski settled down in his favorite armchair and read the latest articles about science. The children gathered around their father's big desk to do their homework.

One day when Manya was about five, she began to wander around the workroom. It was fun to look at all the treasures. Well, maybe not the picture of the bishop. She didn't like that too much. But she loved the fat green clock on the desk. It felt so smooth and cool beneath her fingers. So did the checkerboard table. All the squares were made of marble.

At last she stopped in front of a glass case. Inside were little scales and glass tubes, funny-looking rocks and a mysterious gold machine. Manya didn't know why the items fascinated her, but they did.

"Physics apparatus," her father told her.

"Physics apparatus." The words echoed round and round in Manya's head. Soon she had turned them into a little song. Such strange-sounding words! But somehow wonderful, too.

Little Manya didn't know then how important those words would be to her later in life.

Chapter 2

HARD TIMES

Manya grew into a small, quiet girl. Her pale blond curls bounced around her face, except when they were twisted into a tight braid for school. But her gray eyes were serious and her skin was very white.

Times were not easy in Poland. But sometimes it seemed as if life was especially hard for Manya Sklodowska and her family.

The first really bad thing that happened was that Mrs. Sklodowska and Zosia went off to Nice for a year. The family hoped that the sunshine and warm weather there would help Mrs. Sklodowska feel better.

"After her cure, Mama will be altogether well," the grown-ups told Manya.

But Nice was so far away—all the way to southern France. And a year was such a long time to be without Mama and Zosia.

The year passed and the travelers came home again. Manya could see at once that Mama wasn't altogether well. In fact, Mama looked much worse than when she had left. She was so changed that Manya almost didn't recognize her.

But the family struggled on together. The children tried

to help as much as they could and Professor Sklodowski tried to hide his worried frowns. Many of the Sklodowski's relatives lived in the country. So the family usually spent summer vacations visiting them.

They had just returned from a vacation in 1873 when another bad thing happened. Professor Sklodowski found an envelope on his desk. Inside was a letter telling him that he and his family no longer could live at the boys' high school. He wasn't to be the underinspector of the school any longer. And he wouldn't earn as much money.

Mr. Ivanov, the director, had never liked Professor Sklodowski. He thought the professor didn't show him enough respect. He had been waiting and watching for a chance to get the professor in trouble. That chance had come. Mr. Ivanov had won.

Sadly, the Sklodowskis left their apartment. They moved several times before they finally settled in a new home. It was a big apartment on the corner of Novolipki and Carmelite streets. Professor Sklodowski was so worried about money now that he took yet another job. He became a landlord.

He invited two or three of his young students to live at his home. In return for the money they paid, the boys got a home, food, and some private lessons with the professor.

Soon, though, there were ten boys in the apartment. Ten boys make a lot of noise and also take up a lot of room. Before long, Manya found herself sleeping on a couch in the dining room. It was the only place left for her. Furthermore, she had to be up and out of the dining room by six each morning. That was when the boys ate breakfast.

Manya tried to be cheerful about this. After all, it wasn't the boys' fault. They had to have their breakfast. It wasn't the boys' fault either that her sisters Bronya and Zosia caught typhus from one of them.

Typhus was a terrible disease. Its victims burned with fever and ached all over. Doctors couldn't do much to help them in those days, and many victims died of the disease.

For weeks Bronya and Zosia fought their dreadful battle. Finally Bronya began to get better. But Zosia grew weaker and weaker. One day in 1876 she died.

Pale and trembling, Manya went with Joseph, Hela, and her father to see her big sister for the last time. She stared at the slender figure, dressed all in white, lying on a bier. How beautiful Zosia looked! She even seemed to be smiling. Surely she couldn't be dead.

But she was. Later Manya followed the funeral procession down the street. She shivered in her little black coat. If only Mama could be with her! Or Bronya. But Bronya was still too weak to leave her bed. And Mama—well, she was still sick, too. Between spasms of coughing, she leaned at the window and watched her daughter's coffin pass from view.

Of course, some good things did happen during those

years. One of the people who worked hard to make them happen was Manya's Aunt Lucia. Whenever she could, Aunt Lucia took Manya and Hela for little trips in the fresh air. They weren't marvelously exciting trips. Sometimes Aunt Lucia just took the girls down to the river to buy apples from a man on a boat. But it *was* good to get out in the crisp air.

There was another sort of trip that Manya liked even better, though—a trip into a book. Most of all, she liked to settle herself at the dining room table with a book. She liked all kinds of books—poetry, adventure stories, and even big, heavy technical books that belonged to her father.

Once Manya began reading, nothing could bother her. She even forgot about her sister Hela being there in the room with her. That wasn't easy to do, because Hela always learned her lessons by yelling them as loud as she could.

One evening, Aunt Lucia's daughter, Henrietta, was visiting the family. As usual, Manya was bent over a book at the table. Her sisters and cousin decided to play a trick on her. Carefully they built a pyramid of six chairs all around Manya. It was an extremely shaky pyramid and they couldn't keep from giggling. But Manya didn't notice a thing.

Finally she finished a chapter and sat up straight. CRASH! Chairs tumbled down all around her. Bewildered, Manya looked at Hela, who was screaming with laughter. Henrietta and Bronya seemed a little worried, though. They thought Manya would really be upset.

But Manya wasn't at all angry. Calmly she picked up her book and started for another room.

"That's stupid," she said to the girls.

School was another pleasant experience for Manya—at least most of the time. She went to Miss Sikorska's private school. The school had an endless number of rules and regulations, as did most schools at the time. Each day Manya sat at her desk next to Hela. All the girls wore dark uniforms with white starched collars and steel buttons. Their hair was pulled back tightly into braids.

Miss Tupalska taught Manya's class. She was an ugly woman and sometimes she had to be strict with Manya, who could be stubborn. But the girls all liked her. They had nicknamed her Tupsia.

Manya was two years younger than the rest of her classmates. She had been promoted quickly because she learned so easily. But she had no trouble in this class of older girls. Again and again she scored first in arithmetic, literature, history, German, French, and religion.

History classes were especially exciting. The people who ran Manya's school hated the Russians as much as most other Poles did. Whenever they could, they broke the rules and taught the girls the history of Poland—in the Polish language.

Of course they never knew when a Russian inspector might show up to observe the classes. So they figured out an early-warning system. As soon as an inspector arrived at the front door, the janitor rang a secret signal on an electric bell. Two long rings, two short rings.

Quick as a flash, Tupsia grabbed all the Polish books and papers and gave them to four girls who lived at the school. The four girls streaked to their sleeping quarters and hid the forbidden material. A moment later they were back at their desks. When the inspector opened the classroom door, all he saw was twenty-five girls busily sewing while their teacher read to them from a book of Russian fairy tales.

Sometimes the inspector asked Tupsia to call on one of the girls. That girl then had to answer the inspector's questions—in Russian. Most of the time Tupsia called on Manya. She wasn't picking on her. Manya simply knew more than the others. And she spoke Russian beautifully.

But Manya dreaded those moments. Once she had to recite the Lord's Prayer in Russian, besides answering a lot of questions about Russian history. Saying the prayer—the prayer that meant so much to the Polish people—in that other language seemed the most dreadful task of all.

After the inspector left, Tupsia called Manya up to her and kissed her on the forehead. Manya burst into tears. She wasn't crying because she was afraid of the inspector. She was crying because she hated him and all the awful things he and his government were doing to her people.

Even during the good times, though, Manya knew that the

worst thing of all was still waiting to happen. Each day her mother grew worse. Finally, on May 7, 1878, Mrs. Sklodowska sent for her priest. After she had spent some time with him, she asked to see her family. Quietly the professor and the four children filed into the room and gathered around the bed.

Mrs. Sklodowska said good-bye to each of them. That took almost all the strength she had left. But she found just a little more, raised her hand, and made the sign of the cross.

"I love you," she said very softly and died.

Manya was only ten years old when her mother died. Her father tried to fill the gap. He hired a housekeeper to run their home. He talked with his children, told them Polish folktales, and read to them. He was an excellent father. But he was not a mother.

Manya never complained. Inside, though, she felt lost and miserable. She felt angry, too—angry at God and angry at life for being so cruel.

Chapter 3

GROWING UP

When Manya was a young girl, people mourned dead relatives a long time. Black curtains hung at the windows. Family members wore black clothing.

The Sklodowski family mourned Mrs. Sklodowska for several years. That was hard on Manya. It seemed as if she would never be able to put away her grief and get on with living. Of course she missed her mother. But she knew, too, that her mother would want her to be happy.

Then, when Manya was fourteen, things began to improve. She enrolled at a government high school. That was the only kind of school permitted to give official diplomas. Some of her teachers were Russians and some were Germans. Manya made fun of them whenever she could get away with it.

Miss Mayer, the woman in charge of studies in general, was Manya's special enemy. She was a tiny woman who scooted around in soft-soled slippers spying on everyone. She was always scolding Manya for something or other. But Manya got even with her by staring at her as innocently as possible. One day Miss Mayer had had enough.

"I forbid you to look at me like that!" she said. "You mustn't look down on me!"

Manya kept right on looking at the furious little teacher, who was a head shorter than she.

"The fact is," she said, "that I can't do anything else."

Some of Manya's teachers were Polish, though, and she practically worshipped them. And—no matter who the teacher was—she enjoyed her classes. Learning was like breathing for her. She *had* to do it. During one summer vacation she wrote to a friend: "Do you know, Kazia, in spite of everything, I like school. Perhaps you will make fun of me, but nevertheless I must tell you that I like it, and even that I love it."

Studying was easier for Manya now. Once again the family had moved, this time to an apartment on Leschen Street. It was big enough for the boy boarders to have their quarters away from the Sklodowski family. No more sleeping in the dining room for Manya! No more listening to the boys groan through their lessons.

She made many friends at high school, but her best friend was a girl named Kazia Przyborovska. Each morning Manya packed her lunch (bread, sausages, and an apple), grabbed her book bag, and ran to Kazia's home. Kazia's father worked for a count and the whole family lived at the count's palace.

The two girls would hurry to school, chattering as fast as they could. After school they walked home together. Sometimes they sloshed through mud puddles, just for the fun of it. Sometimes they played silly games. But their ritual at "the monument" wasn't silly to them at all.

"The monument" had been put up by the Russian tsar in honor of the Poles who were Russia's friends. Manya and Kazia hated it. Each time they passed it, they spat on it. If they happened to forget, they couldn't rest until they had hurried back and done it.

One day at school they learned that someone had assassinated Tsar Alexander II. Manya and Kazia couldn't contain themselves. Gleefully they danced around the room. That got them into trouble with Miss Mayer. But they didn't care. One of their enemies was dead.

This attitude might sound heartless to people who have never had another country take over their homeland. But Manya and her friends had grown up hating their Russian conquerors—and with good reason.

One day when Manya was fifteen, she and Kazia arrived at school to find their friend Leonie in tears. She was so upset that she could hardly speak. But finally she managed to tell them what had happened.

Her older brother had joined a plot against the Russians. Somehow the authorities found out about him. They arrested him and kept him in prison for three days without telling his family where he was. In the morning they were going to hang him.

Manya and Kazia were supposed to go to a dancing lesson

that night. Instead, they went with Bronya, Hela, and Kazia's sister Ula to sit up all night with Leonie.

There was little they could do for her. They cried with her and put cool cloths on her eyes. They made her drink some tea. At dawn, when the dreadful moment came, they knelt with her and prayed. It was an experience none of them could ever forget.

Kazia's parents were fond of Manya. They felt bad because she had no mother and tried to treat her like one of their own children. Sometimes Mrs. Przyborovska invited her to stop by for tea after school. Then she fixed special treats for her.

Kazia was also a welcome guest at the Sklodowski home. Bronya, Hela, and Joseph were old enough now for parties and occasionally invited their friends over for an evening of polkas, mazurkas, waltzes, and other popular dances. Kazia and Manya had learned these dances at school. But they weren't considered old enough yet to dance at the home parties. Instead they had to sit on little chairs and watch. It was very frustrating—but fun, nevertheless.

Then at last the magic moment came—graduation. Manya won a gold medal for outstanding scholarship. That wasn't unusual in her family. Bronya and Joseph had won gold medals, too. Joseph was now studying to be a doctor at the University of Warsaw.

Still, the Sklodowskis were proud of their little Manya.

She looked so dignified in her black graduation dress with roses pinned at the waist. She won other prizes, too—books. But she told everyone the books were "horrible." After all, they were Russian books.

As a reward for all her hard work, Professor Sklodowski decided to let Manya have a whole year's vacation in the country. There were all those relatives she could stay with, so it wouldn't cost much.

That year was one of the happiest times in Manya's life. She slept as late as she wanted to sleep, and when she did get up, she did whatever she wanted to do. She walked in the woods and gathered wild flowers. She swam and fished for shrimp. She played children's games and read silly novels. She stuffed herself with strawberries.

"I can't believe geometry or algebra ever existed," she wrote to Kazia. "I have completely forgotten them."

One of her uncles raised fine horses. At his home, Manya learned to ride. Other relatives lived in the Carpathian Mountains. There she climbed mountains and drank in the beauty of the snowy peaks, quaint cottages, and icy lakes.

Winter was spent in the mountains with an aunt, uncle, and three girl cousins. There Manya learned to have fun as she had never had it before. Every week seemed to be filled with special visitors or a religious holiday or a party.

Best of all, though, were the *kuligs*. Everyone dressed up in fancy peasant costumes for a kulig, a kind of ball or party.

In the evening, horse-drawn sleighs carried Manya and her cousins off across the sparkling snow. Young men holding torches rode alongside them. Soon they met other sleighs and other riders, including musicians, who somehow managed to play their fiddles as they whisked along.

Then the whole group arrived at the home of friends. The friends were expecting them, even though they pretended to be asleep. Everyone trooped inside. The musicians leaped onto a table. The hosts came running with heaping trays of food. The ball began.

Suddenly someone gave a signal and everyone rushed for the sleighs again. Off they whizzed to another house and another ball. On and on they went for two days and two nights. Dancers and musicians grabbed a little sleep whenever they absolutely had to—but only then. After each ball the crowd grew larger. On the second night, they all ended up at the biggest house in the neighborhood for the best ball of all.

Finally, though, Manya's vacation came to an end—or so she thought. But she had barely gotten home when the Countess de Fleury came to see her father. This woman had been one of Mrs. Sklodowska's pupils years before. Now she wanted to do something nice for her former teacher's daughters. The next day Manya and Hela were on their way to the countess's country house at Kempa. They were to stay at least two months.

In a letter to Kazia, Manya said that life at Kempa was "marvelous." She swam and learned to row. She danced, rode, and got into mischief with the other young people staying there. The countess and her husband pretended to be stern. But secretly they were having as much fun as everyone else.

Once Manya decided to play a trick on the countess's brother. While he was busy on an errand in town, she talked the other young people into helping her hang everything in his room—including the furniture—from the ceiling. The poor man didn't get home until after dark—and was he confused!

The countess did her part to add to the fun. In only two months she held three balls, two garden parties, and took the young people on many trips by land and water. The young people decided to repay her and her husband for their hospitality by doing something special for them on their fourteenth wedding anniversary. They made them a huge crown of vegetables that weighed forty pounds. While the astonished couple were trying to figure out what to do with this gift, someone read a poem that Manya had written. It ended up asking for another party! And of course the de Fleurys gave one.

At last, though, it was time for Manya to go back home to Warsaw and think about her future. Both she and Bronya wanted more than anything to go on studying, as Joseph was doing. But women were not allowed to attend the University of Warsaw, and they couldn't afford to go away to some other university.

Again and again Professor Sklodowski blamed himself. If he hadn't lost his savings in a bad investment some years before, he would now be able to send his daughters abroad for a good education. But again and again his children told him not to worry. They would do just fine.

There weren't many ways young people could earn money in those days in Poland. About all they could do was some private tutoring. So that's what Manya and Bronya did. Through all kinds of weather they tramped to the homes of their pupils. Sometimes the pupils' parents forgot to pay them. It wasn't an easy job, but they hung on stubbornly.

They did manage to have some good times. A number of young people in Warsaw decided to start a "floating university." At meetings in private homes, lectures were given on such subjects as anatomy, natural history, and sociology. It was definitely illegal. Those who attended could have been thrown into prison if the authorities ever found out. But Manya and Bronya didn't let that stop them. Women were welcome at the floating university, so they went.

Manya even became a teacher for the university. Whenever she could, she read aloud to a group of women who worked for a small dressmaking business. Soon she had put together a small library of books in Polish for the women.

Manya (left) and Bronya as young students

Her father was a good model for her in this work. He was still reading aloud to his family, mostly books by Polish romantic writers. Some of these books had been banned by the tsar. But somehow Professor Sklodowski got hold of them.

Manya still read on her own, too. She spent hours in her room, deep into books written by people from all over the world. She was beginning to dream some dreams now. Wouldn't it be wonderful to go to Paris and study at the Sorbonne? Wouldn't it be wonderful to find a way to make life better for her people in Poland?

Then something happened to make Manya put away her dreams for a while.

Chapter 4

THE WAITING DREAMS

Manya herself made that something happen. Yes, she had her dreams. But Bronya also had dreams. She wanted to go to Paris as much as Manya did. There she would study medicine. When she became a doctor, she would come back to Poland and help people who lived in the country.

But so far all Bronya could do was take care of the Sklodowski home. There was no money to send her to Paris. That bothered Manya terribly. So one day she came up with a plan.

Bronya had saved enough money to get to Paris and live there for a year. If Manya could get a job as a governess, she would be able to help Bronya through the remaining four years it took to become a doctor. Maybe she would even be able to put some money aside for her own education.

At first Bronya said no to this plan—absolutely no. Why should she get to go when Manya wanted the same thing just as much? But Manya had some practical arguments on her side. She was only seventeen. She had lots of time ahead of her. Bronya, on the other hand, was twenty. Besides, once Bronya became a doctor, she could help Manya get her education.

Finally Bronya gave in. So one day in September of 1885,

Manya dressed herself to look as much like a governess as possible and went to an employment agency. In almost no time she had a job.

That first job was with a family of lawyers in Warsaw. Manya hated it. Her employers were rich. But they were also stupid, stingy, and cruel. Manya's own family had always been warm and loving. She couldn't get used to a home in which people were hypocritical and dishonest to one another and cut one another to bits with unkind words.

She also discovered that being a governess in Warsaw had its drawbacks. True, she could see her family and friends sometimes. But she wasn't saving enough money. She would be able to save a lot more if she worked for a family in the country.

By January of 1886, she had quit her first job and begun working for the Zorawski family. They lived at a place called Szczuki, north of Warsaw. It took Manya three hours by train plus four hours by sleigh to get there. She cried a great deal during her journey. It was hard to leave family and friends behind and set off on her own. But at least she would be in the country, she told herself. She had always loved the country.

Manya arrived at Szczuki at night. It wasn't until the next morning that she realized what a mistake she'd made. Mr. Zorawski raised beets and refined them into sugar. When Manya looked out her window that first morning, all she could see were red brick factory buildings and beet fields. Dirty, smoky buildings and miles and miles of beet fields. Some people might have cried from disappointment. But not Manya. She laughed.

In time, she found some good things at Szczuki. Mr. Zorawski was kind to her. Mrs. Zorawska had a bit of a temper, but Manya managed to get along with her. The older three Zorawski boys were at school in Warsaw, but three-year-old Stas kept everyone in stitches. Baby Maryshna was only six months old. Then there were Manya's two pupils—Andzia, age ten, and Bronka, age eighteen. She spent four hours each day teaching Andzia and three teaching Bronka. Andzia could be troublesome at times, but Bronka and Manya soon became fast friends.

Having the factory there wasn't all bad either. At least she could borrow books from its library. And she had a big, pleasant room with a private entrance. She could study to her heart's content during her few spare hours.

Those spare hours became even fewer before long. One day Manya met some ragged little peasant children on the road. Their parents worked for Mr. Zorawski. As she looked at them, Manya remembered one of her dreams—to make life better for the Polish people. Why not start with these children?

She went to the Zorawskis with a plan. What about starting a little school for the children? It would meet for only a few hours each week. But during that time she could teach the children some Polish history and how to read and write the language. Bronka wanted to help.

Of course such a plan was illegal. If the Russians found out, everyone involved would be in serious trouble. But Mr. Zorawski told Manya to go ahead—as long as she held the school in her own room.

Soon eighteen peasant children were trooping up to Manya's room. Most days she spent two hours with them. But on Wednesdays and Saturdays she could give them five hours. The children found it very difficult to learn. After all, they had little experience doing it. But Manya persisted and finally the day came when all her pupils could read and write their native language. Manya didn't know who was proudest—the children, their parents (who couldn't read and write themselves), or she herself—their triumphant teacher.

Manya was doing important work as a governess and teacher. Still, secretly, she wanted only one thing—to go on studying. Literature and sociology fascinated her. But she knew now that her real interest lay in mathematics and physics. Those magic words from her childhood—"physics apparatus"—came back to her. It was difficult to learn physics on her own, though, especially since she didn't have a laboratory. All she could do was struggle on, waiting and hoping that her brain wouldn't forget what it knew already.

Then something happened that made even the waiting seem impossible. The Zorawskis' oldest son, Casimir, came home from the university for a vacation. He was just a little older than Manya—and very handsome. In no time the two young people fell in love. Soon they began talking about marriage.

It would be just perfect, Manya thought. Bronka was already like a sister to her. And Mr. and Mrs. Zorawski had always been so kind. They even gave her flowers and presents for her birthday. Sometimes they invited Professor Sklodowski, Joseph, and Hela to visit at Szczuki. What could be more right than uniting the two families with a marriage?

Casimir went to tell his parents about the plans. At once Mr. Zorawski had a temper tantrum. Mrs. Zorawska came close to fainting. Casimir, their beloved oldest son, marry this—this *nobody*? Impossible! He was meant to marry somebody much better, much richer.

Some young men would stand up to their parents in such a situation. But not Casimir Zorawski. He wasn't strong enough. He didn't want to hurt Manya. But hurting Manya would be better than angering his parents.

Manya *was* hurt. She was so hurt that she didn't know what to say. So she said nothing. Silence settled around her like an icy cloak. She wrote to her cousin Henrietta that love would have no more place in her life.

The whole incident would have been much easier for Manya if she could have left the Zorawskis and found another job. It was awful being stranded out in the country with people who didn't think she was good enough for their son. But her contract still had a while to run—and she needed the money. She was sending almost half of her salary to Bronya in Paris every month. She couldn't stop doing that. So she kept working, quietly and grimly.

During those difficult days, she wrote many letters to her family and tried to forget her own troubles by worrying about theirs. Joseph wanted to be a doctor in Warsaw. But he didn't have enough money to do that. Frantically Manya tried to figure out ways to get the money for him. Then there was Henrietta. She was married now, but her child had been born dead. Manya tried to comfort her.

Hela needed comforting, too. Her fiance had broken off their engagement. "Truly it gives one a good opinion of men!" Manya wrote sarcastically to Joseph. "If they don't want to marry poor young girls, let them go to the devil!"

Time dragged on, sad and gray. Manya had been a governess for three years now. She could see no hope of anything better in her future.

"I was barely eighteen when I came here," she wrote to Henrietta, "and what I have not been through! There have been moments which I shall certainly count among the most cruel of my life."

Still, changes were beginning to happen, changes that would touch Manya. Her father had to retire from his high school job. But he found another, as director of a reform school near Warsaw. It was hard, unpleasant work. But it paid well.

Now the professor could send money to Bronya. Manya didn't have to send any more. She could work at building up her own savings. Bronya's studies were going well, too. And she was in love with a Polish medical student whose name was Casimir Dluski.

In the spring of 1889, Manya's contract with the Zorawskis ran out. At once she found another position as a governess. Her new family spent the summer by the Baltic Sea. But in the autumn they returned to Warsaw. Once again Manya was able to see her family and friends.

Then, one March day in 1890, she got a letter from Bronya. Bronya's fiance would soon be a doctor, and she herself had only a year to go. In a few weeks they would be married. If Manya wanted to, she could come to Paris, begin her studies, and live with them.

Suddenly Manya got cold feet. Her father needed her. He was growing older and they had planned to live together the following year. She couldn't disappoint him. There were things she wanted to do for Joseph and Hela, too. But the truth was that Manya had been too sad for too long. She couldn't believe that her life would ever again be happy.

She finished her contract as a governess and moved in with her father. The floating university was still operating, and joy of joys, her cousin Joseph had a laboratory where she could do a few experiments.

So Manya went back to giving private lessons, taking care of her family, and studying on her own. In the summer of 1891, she even took a vacation in the Carpathian Mountains. And who should she meet there but Casimir Zorawski!

For a brief moment Manya must have felt hope again. But once more Casimir explained that he wasn't sure he could marry her. Finally Manya had had enough.

"If you can't see a way to clear up our situation," she told him, "it is not for me to teach it to you."

This final meeting with Casimir was the last straw for Manya in another way, too. At last she realized that if she were ever going to do anything about her future, she must do it now. Her dreams had waited long enough.

She wrote to Bronya: "Decide if you can really take me in at your house, for I can come now. I have enough to pay all my expenses."

The reply came quickly and Manya soon found herself sitting on the hard bench of the cheapest train compartment available. Around her was stacked her luggage, including enough food for the three-day journey. Her cheeks were flushed and her eyes glowed. Manya Sklodowska was on her way to Paris at last.

Chapter 5

LIVING THE DREAM

At the Gare du Nord, a train station in Paris, it was not Manya who got off the train. It was Marie Sklodowska. She was beginning a new life with a new first name, a French name. And what a new life it promised to be! In the streets she could hear people speaking whatever language they preferred. In bookshops she saw heaps of books from all over the world. This was Paris, a free city in a free country. At last she, Marie Sklodowska, was free, too.

To make matters better still, her beloved sister Bronya and her new brother-in-law Casimir were ready to give her a home and their love. Both the Dluskis were doctors now and had their office in their apartment. During part of the day, Casimir used it to see his patients. Then it was Bronya's turn. She worked mostly with women and their diseases.

Both doctors also spent a lot of time visiting patients at their homes. In fact, both were very busy people. But that didn't stop them from having good times. Bronya cooked like a master and kept the apartment bright with flowers. Casimir, a handsome man with black eyes and a black beard, could play the piano and said terribly funny things. Their friends flocked around them. On one evening they all went to the theater. On another they set out for a concert. On yet another—when no one happened to have much money—they stayed at home, sang, and drank countless cups of tea.

In some ways, Marie must have felt that she hadn't left Poland at all. A lot of Poles came to Paris during those years. Some, like Marie, came to study. Others came to escape political troubles at home. All of them, though, felt a strong need to hold on to their Polish roots. They spent a great deal of time together. They even had relatives back home buy certain things—such as tea—and ship them to Paris.

But when Marie stood in front of a cluster of grand old buildings in the heart of the city, she knew she wasn't back home. This was the Sorbonne, the university of her dreams. And she was welcome.

In those days, students at the Sorbonne chose an area or two in which they were interested. Then they looked at the long list of lectures and decided which ones to attend. Marie's areas, of course, were physics and mathematics. She wished she could attend every single lecture given by every one of the twenty-three professors on her list. There was so much that she wanted to learn!

As a matter of fact, there was more to learn than she had expected. Back in Poland, everyone thought her French was excellent. But here in Paris, she discovered that people spoke the language more quickly. Sometimes she missed whole sentences in the lectures. That would never do. She decided to work until she knew the language perfectly.

Most of Marie's training in higher physics and mathematics had come from books studied on her own while she was working as a governess. Now she found out that the students who had gone to French schools knew more than she did. She decided to get more books and catch up with those French students as fast as she could.

None of this hard work bothered Marie in the least. She especially loved the time she could now spend in laboratories. Finally she could get her hands on all that wonderful "physics apparatus." And finally there were professors to show her how to use it.

Marie didn't even mind the long bus rides to and from the Sorbonne each day. She rode on the open top deck of a double-decker omnibus pulled by three horses. It could get pretty cold and wet up there. But what did she care? The fare was cheaper for seats up top. Besides, in only an hour she'd be sitting in a lecture room, listening to some wise man in full evening dress tell her all the things she had always wanted to know.

Only one thing bothered Marie after she had been in Paris for a while. She didn't have enough time to study. Evening parties and theater trips were fine for Bronya and Casimir. They had their degrees and they worked hard all day. They deserved some fun. But Marie needed to spend her evenings with her books. That wasn't easy with a crowd of people singing and laughing in the next room.

So Marie talked with the Dluskis and came up with a plan. She would move to a cheap room in the Latin Quarter, a section of Paris near the Sorbonne. Paying rent and buying her own food would leave her very poor. But at least she would avoid bus fares, since she could walk to the university. And she would have all the time and quiet she needed for studying.

Marie lived in several different rooms during her time at the Sorbonne. In many ways they were all alike. They were all small, dark, bare, cold in winter, hot in summer—and cheap. She brought her own furnishings with her. There was a folding iron bed and mattress, a white wooden table and chair, a small stove for heating, an oil lamp, an alcohol heater for cooking, a washbasin, and a pitcher for water brought from downstairs. Her rooms didn't have running water. If she needed an extra seat for a guest, there was always the wooden trunk brought from Poland. For kitchenware she had two plates, three glasses, a cup, a kettle, a pan, a knife, a fork, and a spoon.

Marie's room was usually near the top of a house. That meant she had to haul coal for her stove up flight after flight of stairs. Not that she bought much coal anyway. She couldn't afford it. Besides, she could always spend her evenings at a library where it was warm and bright. Of course libraries closed at ten and she usually studied till two. But Polish girls were used to hard winters. And when she finally did crawl into bed, she could pile all her clothes on top of the blanket to help keep her warm. Once she even piled the kitchen chair on top of the clothes. At least it *felt* warm.

Marie's main problem was food. She had learned a lot of things during her short life, but never how to cook. "Miss Sklodowska doesn't know what you use to make soup," her Polish friends in Paris told one another.

They were right. She didn't. So most of the time she ate bread and butter and drank tea. Sometimes she bought fresh fruit or a bunch of radishes. Sometimes she simply forgot to eat at all.

One day Marie fainted in front of one of her friends. The friend ran to get Casimir. After Casimir checked Marie over, he looked around her room. He found no food—only a packet of tea. Casimir was furious.

"When did you eat today?" he asked his sister-in-law.

Marie had trouble remembering. It finally turned out that she had eaten nothing but a few radishes and some cherries since the evening before. And *that* meal hadn't been much either.

Casimir told her to pack up what she'd need for a week. Then he took her home to Bronya. They were barely through the front door when Bronya got busy in the kitchen. For the next week, Marie ate and rested like a normal human being at the Dluskis'. At the end of the week she promised her sister and brother-in-law to take better care of herself in the future. So they let her go home—to bread and butter and tea.

At last, in the summer of 1893, the time came for Marie to take her examinations for the master's degree in physics. Could she pass? Had all her hard work been enough? She had to wait for days after the exams to find out.

Then, crowded in a room with fellow students and their families, she heard the examiner read the results. She had passed! Not only that, her marks were the highest of all. Marie didn't wait for congratulations. Instead, she rushed to get ready for a well-deserved vacation—in Poland.

Her family was delighted to see her. Professor Sklodowski, Joseph, and Hela had all missed her while she was gone. To show their love, they fed her and then fed her some more. She was nothing but a skinny little waif now! Didn't people eat in Paris? Well, they would fatten her up!

Meanwhile, Marie's mind was busy, rushing ahead toward the next dream. True, she had a master's degree in physics. However, she wanted a second one in mathematics. But how was she to get it? The same old problem—money—haunted her. Her own savings were dwindling fast. And she hated to ask her father for more help. He had given up so much for her already.

Then Marie got a big surprise. In Paris she had become friends with a Polish girl, Miss Dydynska, who was studying

44

mathematics. Miss Dydynska had returned to Poland for the summer, too. She believed that Marie would do great things some day. She also knew how to pull strings in the right places. Thanks to her, the Alexandrovitch Scholarship was awarded to Marie.

The scholarship was worth six hundred rubles. It meant that Marie could go back to Paris for another fifteen months. She could get a master's degree in mathematics. In no time at all she was on her way.

(Several years later, Marie saved up six hundred rubles from money she earned. She took the money to the secretary of the Alexandrovitch Foundation to pay back her scholarship. The secretary just stared at her. Nobody had *ever* paid back a scholarship to the foundation before. But Marie insisted. Some other young girl might need that money as much as she once had.)

Back in Paris, Marie at once found another cheap room and resumed studying. All in all, she lived the life of a poor student for four years. For many people it would have been a miserable life. But Marie felt she was doing what she had been born to do. She was living one of her dearest dreams. And there is no better feeling than that.

Chapter 6

NEW BEGINNINGS

While Marie was studying for the master's degree in mathematics, she was suddenly made to feel like a real scientist. The Society for the Encouragement of National Industry asked her to prepare a study of the magnetic properties of various steels. This meant that she would have to analyze different kinds of minerals and metals.

At first her physics professor, Gabriel Lippmann, said she could do the work in his laboratory. But the job took a large amount of equipment and Marie soon saw she would need more room. She mentioned the problem to some friends of hers, the Kowalskis. Joseph Kowalski thought he had an answer.

Joseph knew a physicist who worked at the School of Physics and Chemistry. This man might have an extra room in which Marie could work. Joseph and his wife invited the man to their home the next evening to meet Marie. The man's name was Pierre Curie.

Marie and Pierre liked each other at once. She was flattered because Pierre, who was already a respected scientist, actually talked with her about his work. He had made some important discoveries and had even invented a scientific scale. Pierre was surprised and pleased to meet a woman who wanted to hear about his work—and who seemed to understand what he told her.

"Are you going to remain in France always?" he asked her.

"Certainly not," she replied. She told him about her dream of someday going back to Poland to help her people there.

Pierre disagreed with her plans. He thought she should spend her life working for science, not Poland. And, for some reason, he didn't want her to leave France.

At first Marie and Pierre met only at sessions of the Physics Society. Then Pierre sent her a present. He chose something that meant a lot to him and that he knew she would like. It was a copy of his most recently published study: *On Symmetry in Physical Phenomena: Symmetry of an Electric Field and of a Magnetic Field.* On the first page he wrote: "To Mlle. Sklodowska, with the respect and friendship of the author, P. Curie."

None of this was a very romantic beginning to a relationship. But it was exactly right for Marie and Pierre. Both of them loved science more than anything else in the world. Both had been hurt by someone when they were very young and had sworn never to fall in love again.

Even so, Pierre, who was thirty-five, wanted to get to know Marie still better. He asked if he could visit her. She said he could. For the first time he saw the poor little room where she worked so hard.

Months went by and they continued to see one another. Marie discovered that she had something to give Pierre, too—encouragement. He needed someone to tell him to write up the experiments he was doing and to urge him to study for a doctor's degree.

One day Pierre introduced Marie to his parents, who reminded her of her own family. She liked them at once. They didn't seem to think she was strange either, working so hard at being a scientist.

In the summer of 1894, Marie passed another important set of examinations and earned a master's degree in mathematics. This meant that she soon would be traveling back to Poland for the summer. Pierre didn't know if she would return to Paris again. So he gathered his courage and asked her to marry him.

Marie turned him down. She liked Pierre and she wanted to be friends with him. But she couldn't leave her family in Poland forever. Nor could she give up her dream of doing something for the Polish people. In no time she was on the train and gone, leaving a sad Pierre behind.

But he didn't give up. Instead he wrote letter after letter to her. He wrote about their friendship. He wrote about "our dreams: *your* patriotic dream, *our* humanitarian dream, and *our* scientific dream." And over and over again he begged her to come back to Paris in the autumn.

Marie answered many of his letters. But she didn't send

the news that he wanted to hear until September. Then she wrote that, yes, she would be coming back. With that letter she sent him a picture of herself. Pierre showed the picture to his brother Jacques. Jacques said that Marie looked like a stubborn person. As if Pierre didn't already know!

Once she was back in Paris, though, it might be easier to get her to change her mind and marry him. He certainly intended to try. First he suggested that they simply share an apartment—as friends. They could divide it in two and each use half to work in. That didn't sound like a very good idea to Marie. Then he suggested that he could go to Poland and get a job there—maybe teaching French. Marie would never let him make such a sacrifice for her. But she was deeply touched by his willingness to do it.

Finally Pierre went to Bronya and asked for her help. He even had his mother talk to Bronya.

"There isn't a soul on earth to equal my Pierre," said his mother.

By this time Bronya was all for the marriage. But she couldn't rush her little sister. It took ten more months of patience and love before Marie finally gave Pierre her "yes."

"I am about to marry the man I told you about last year in Warsaw," she wrote to her old friend Kazia. "It is a sorrow to me to have to stay forever in Paris, but what am I to do? Fate has made us deeply attached to each other and we cannot endure the idea of separating."

On July 26, 1895, Marie put on a new outfit, a navy blue suit and a blue-striped blouse. Casimir Dluski's mother had given it to her. It was to be her wedding dress. Pierre came by for her, and together they rode on the top deck of an omnibus to the train station. What a change from those cold wet rides when she had first come to Paris!

The train took them to Sceaux, where Pierre's parents lived. Other visitors waited there for them—Bronya and Casimir, some friends from the university, and Professor Sklodowski and Hela, who had come all the way from Warsaw for their little Manya's wedding.

The wedding itself took place at the city hall in Sceaux. Then there was a party in the Curie family's garden. A cousin in Poland had sent Marie money to buy a wedding present. Most women would have bought linens or dishes or a piece of furniture for the new home. But not Marie. She bought two bicycles—one for her, one for Pierre. Soon after the wedding, they hopped onto the bicycles and set off on their honeymoon.

Each day they pedaled along French country roads. When they felt like it, they got off their bikes and rambled through the woods. When they were hungry, they ate bread, cheese, and fruit in some woodland clearing. When night fell, they stopped at an inn and ate a supper of good hot soup.

It was an odd kind of honeymoon, a mixture of romance and science, of being together and being alone in their own

Pierre and Marie Curie with their bicycles in the French countryside

thoughts. When Pierre became very silent, Marie didn't worry. She knew he was puzzling over his work back in Paris. She had plenty to think about, too. Next year she was going to enter a fellowship competition at the university.

One day they found a lovely little pond hidden in some woods. Marie lay down on the bank and Pierre crept carefully out onto a log. He was going to pick some irises and water lilies for her. Marie's eyes were closed and her hand was open when he got back. But her eyes opened fast when she felt something cold, wet, and heavy plopped down on her hand. It was a frog.

"Really, Pierre!" said Marie. She sounded frightened.

Pierre couldn't understand. Didn't she *like* frogs? He'd always liked them. They were such nice, amusing creatures.

It was an odd kind of honeymoon, but as far as Marie and Pierre Curie were concerned, a perfect one.

Around the middle of August, they parked their bicycles at an old farmhouse near Chantilly. Bronya had rented it for the summer. There Pierre and Marie stayed for a while with Bronya, Casimir, the Dluskis' three-year-old daughter Helen, Casimir's mother, and—best of all—Professor Sklodowski and Hela, who were remaining in France a little longer. Sometimes Pierre's parents also came to visit. It was a glorious family party. Pierre adored his new in-laws and even tried to learn to speak Polish.

Then, in September, it was Marie's turn to stay with *her* in-laws at the house at Sceaux. She already knew that she loved Pierre's mother and father (who was a doctor). Didn't they remind her of her own family? But now she also built a warm friendship with Pierre's older brother, Jacques, another physicist.

At last, though, the time came for the young Curies to return to Paris, to their work, and to the little flat they had rented at 24 Rue de la Glacière. They had a new life to begin—a life together.

Marie Curie as a young woman

Above:
Pierre and Marie Curie

Right:
Marie with her
daughters, Ève (left)
and Irène

Marie and Pierre Curie in their laboratory in 1906, shortly before Pierre's death

Marie Curie in her laboratory at the Institute of Radium

Marie Curie's daughter Irène worked with her during World War I, and then became her assistant at the Institute of Radium in Paris (above). Irène and her husband, Frédéric Joliot, who were married in 1926, received the Nobel Prize in chemistry in 1935, the year after Marie Curie died.

Marie Curie with four of her students

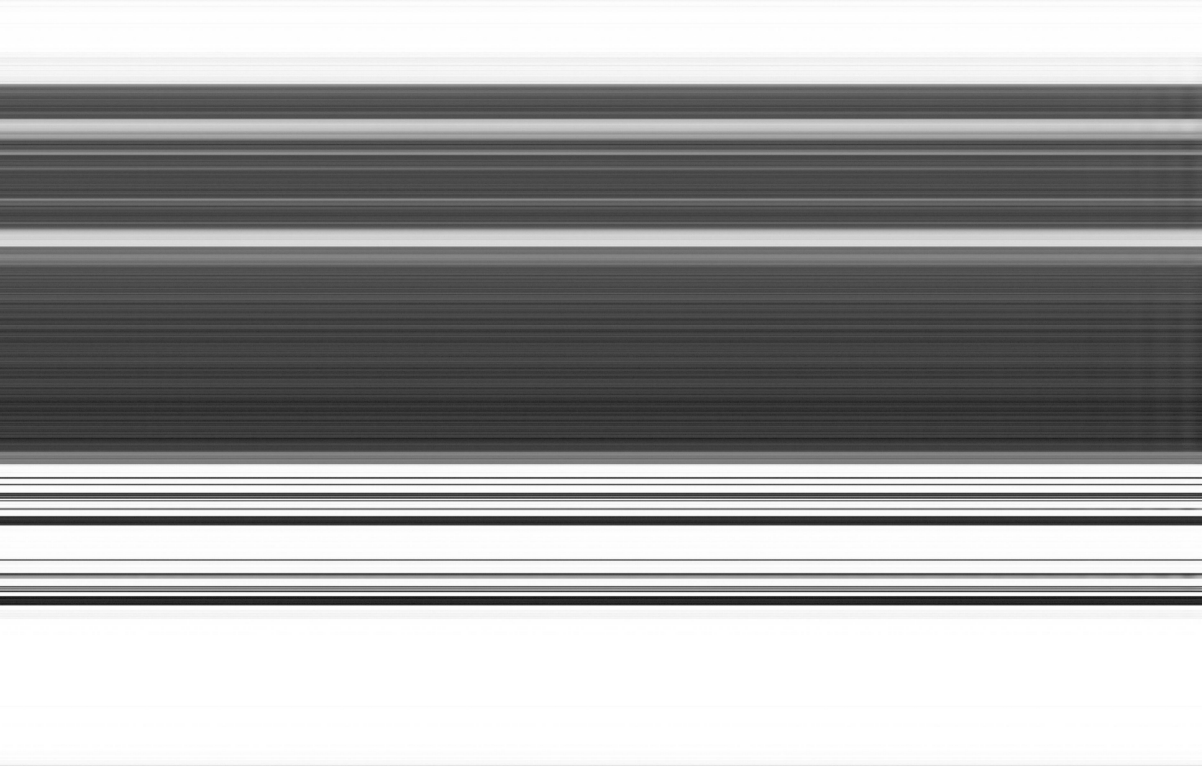

urie poses with President
during her 1921 trip to the
accept a gift from the
of one gram of radium for

nd trip to the United States,
Herbert Hoover
with another gift from the
e, a gram of radium for the
um in Warsaw.

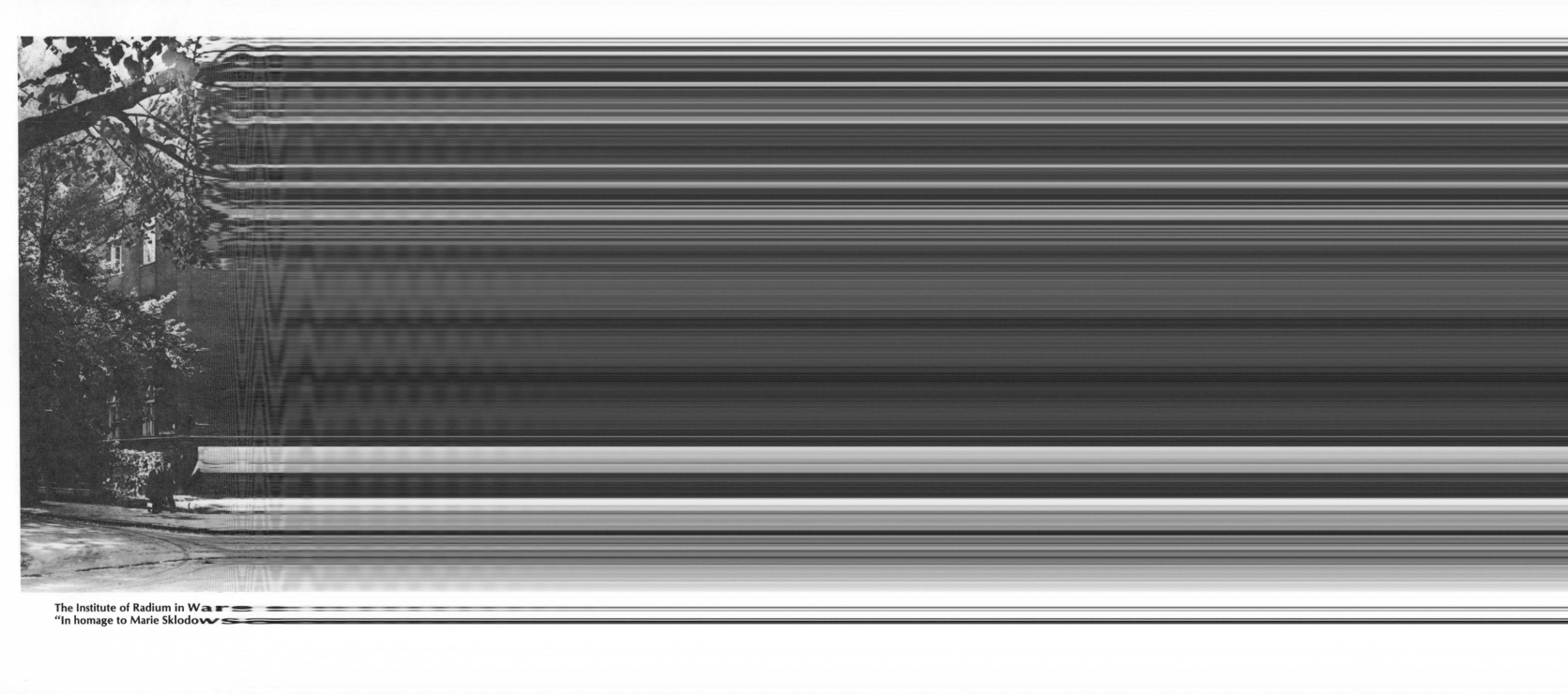

The Institute of Radium in Wars
"In homage to Marie Sklodo

Marie Curie's daughter Irène worked with her during World War I, and then became her assistant at the Institute of Radium in Paris (above). Irène and her husband, Frédéric Joliot, who were married in 1926, received the Nobel Prize in chemistry in 1935, the year after Marie Curie died.

Marie Curie with four of her students

Above: Marie Curie poses with President Warren Harding during her 1921 trip to the United States to accept a gift from the American people of one gram of radium for her laboratory.

Left: On a second trip to the United States, in 1929, President Herbert Hoover presented Marie with another gift from the American people, a gram of radium for the Institute of Radium in Warsaw.

The Institute of Radium in Warsaw, Poland carries the inscription:
"In homage to Marie Sklodowska Curie."

Chapter 7

A TIME OF DISCOVERIES

Marie and Pierre Curie did not want a fancy home. They had three little rooms that were quite enough for them. Caring for a fancy home took time and energy. They planned to spend *their* time and energy on science.

One of the three rooms was their office. In it were books, a table, a lamp, and two chairs. Marie worked at one end of the table, Pierre at the other. What more could they need?

They really couldn't have afforded much more anyway. Pierre earned only a small salary at the School of Physics and Chemistry. Marie earned nothing while she studied for the fellowship competition. She had to pass that competition, though, in order to teach in France.

The Curies certainly could not afford a maid to help with the household work. Marie would have to do it herself. But she intended to do it in a way that would take as little time as possible. She would figure out a method—scientifically.

As soon as she knew she was getting married, she had asked Bronya and Casimir's mother to give her cooking lessons. Cooking reminded Marie a lot of chemistry and, as far as she was concerned, it was just as difficult. Patiently she experimented and made careful notes in the margins of her

cookbook. Before long, she knew what to use to make soup. She even began inventing dishes of her own, dishes she could prepare quickly while she was busy with other things. Pierre wasn't the sort of man who noticed what he ate. But she was determined to feed him well.

Marie planned to manage household finances scientifically, too. As soon as she got back from her honeymoon, she bought a black book labeled "Expenses." Inside she made two columns: "Monsieur's Expenditure" and "Madame's Expenditure." In these columns she kept a record of everything they spent.

The instant her household duties were finished, Marie rushed off to her books or her laboratory, where she was still working on her project for the Society for the Encouragement of National Industry. By the time the examinations for the fellowship competition were held, she was ready for them. Once again she passed with a first place. She and Pierre celebrated by taking another bicycle vacation in the country.

The next year, though, Marie discovered a new and happy complication in her life. She was going to have a baby. She wanted the baby very much. But she didn't like feeling sick all the time. It interfered with her work.

The young Curies also had learned that Pierre's mother was dying of cancer. Marie loved Mrs. Curie dearly, so she was as depressed about this as Pierre was.

When the summer of 1897 came, Marie's father traveled from Poland to stay in the country with her. Pierre couldn't leave Paris for a while, although he planned to join them later. Meanwhile, he wrote his wife letters—in Polish—to tell her how much he missed her.

Finally, in August, he was able to go to her. At once the two of them decided to take another bicycle trip, even though Marie was now eight months pregnant. That trip didn't last long. On September 12, Marie was back in Paris and the mother of a baby girl, Irène. Dr. Curie, Pierre's father, delivered his little granddaughter. Pierre's mother lived just long enough to know that the baby had been born.

In the past, many women felt that they had to choose between having a family or having a career. Marie didn't even think about making such a choice. She would have both. She didn't like the idea of hiring a nurse for Irène. But the doctor said she couldn't nurse the child herself. So a nurse was hired and Marie got busy on her project again. Less than three months after Irène's birth, the Society for the Encouragement of National Industry had its study of the magnetic properties of various steels.

About this time, Marie and Pierre moved to a little house in the Boulevard Kellermann. Here their family grew larger. Pierre's father came to live with them. He and baby Irène were already the best of friends. Now he could be with her all the time.

Meanwhile, Marie had a new decision to make. It was time to think about getting a doctor's degree in physics. But she needed a subject for her thesis. So she thought and read and listened to other physicists. And at last she had an idea.

A French scientist, Henri Becquerel, had discovered that uranium gave out rays, even in absolute darkness. It was as if uranium contained some secret sort of energy. But where did that energy come from? What was it like? Those two questions became the subject of Marie's thesis.

Once again she had to find a place to work. Pierre talked to the head of his school and managed to get her a little storeroom. It was damp, uncomfortable, and often cold. But Marie turned it into her laboratory.

First she tried to find out how strong the uranium rays were. To measure them, she used equipment that Pierre and his brother Jacques had invented. The more uranium in the samples, she discovered, the stronger the rays. It didn't matter what other substances the uranium was mixed with. The temperature didn't matter either—nor the amount of light.

Marie became more and more excited. The rays were like nothing anyone else had studied before. Did they exist only in uranium? Or could she find them in other elements? Carefully she began studying all the known chemical elements. Eventually she found the same strange energy in another one—thorium. It was time to give the energy a name. She called it radioactivity.

Next she examined different samples of minerals. She was almost certain what she would find. The minerals that contained uranium or thorium would be radioactive. The minerals that didn't contain those elements wouldn't be radioactive. She was right.

But then she made an extremely surprising discovery. She should have been able to predict how strong the radioactivity would be by the amount of uranium or thorium in her samples. But she couldn't. The radioactivity was always much stronger than she expected it to be.

Why? she asked herself. Had she made a mistake in her experiments? She ran them again and again just to be sure. But the results were always the same. The radioactivity was stronger.

That meant her minerals must contain some element that was even more radioactive than uranium or thorium. But what could it be? She had already examined all the known elements. There was just one answer—a new element.

Finding a new element must be one of the most exciting discoveries a scientist can make. Marie's imagination was in a whirl. At first she told only Pierre and Bronya about her suspicion. Then, on April 12, 1898, she announced in a scientific article that the element *probably* existed.

Scientists are careful people. Marie couldn't just *believe* the element was there. She had to prove it. She had to separate it from other elements and study it. Until now, Pierre had talked with her about her work. Now he decided to help her with it. Soon it became *their* work. At last they were living their scientific dream together.

They discovered that an ore called pitchblende was especially radioactive. So it must contain the new element. Patiently they began examining and analyzing samples of pitchblende. There probably wasn't much of the new element in each sample, they thought. Maybe only one one-hundredth part. (Much later they learned that the element was present in only one one-*millionth* part.)

So they separated each element from pitchblende until they were left with only those that were unusually radioactive. Those? Surely there should be just one unusually radioactive element—the new one. Instead there seemed to be two. Did that mean there were *two* new elements? It certainly looked that way.

In July, 1898, the Curies announced the discovery of one of these elements. Marie chose to name the new element polonium as a tribute to her beloved homeland. She also made certain that an article announcing this discovery appeared in Poland as well as in France.

For the time being, she and Pierre referred to the second radioactive substance as "the other." They thought a lot about it. But summer had come and with it another vacation in the country. This time Irène went along. She was one year old now. With great pride, Marie recorded her daughter's new skills. In August she wrote: "She plays with the cat and chases him with war cries. She is not afraid of strangers any more. She sings a great deal. She gets up on the table when she is in her chair."

There also were sad times in 1898. During that year Casimir and Bronya moved back to Poland, but not to the Russian section. They decided to settle in the area controlled by Austria, where life was a little easier. There they would build a sanatarium for people with tuberculosis.

Marie knew how valuable their work would be. After all, her own mother had died of tuberculosis. But admiration for their work couldn't stop her from missing her beloved sister and brother-in-law.

"You can't imagine what a hole you have made in my life," she wrote to Bronya in December of 1898.

But just a few weeks later in that December—on the twenty-sixth, to be precise—she and Pierre published another piece of research.

"The various reasons we have just enumerated lead us to believe that the new radioactive substance contains a new element to which we propose to give the name of RADIUM."

Chapter 8

MORE BATTLES

Marie and Pierre had made some tremendous discoveries. But in many ways, their work had just begun. Now they had to obtain pure radium and polonium by separating them from pitchblende. They had to compute the atomic weight of the new elements. Only then would other scientists be convinced of the discoveries.

To obtain the pure elements, they would need more pitchblende—a large amount of it. Where to get it? Then they had an unexpected piece of good luck. The Austrian government offered a ton of pitchblende residue, which was exactly what they needed. The Curies would have to pay only the cost of transportation.

Meanwhile, they had to find a place to put all of the ore—and to work with it. The Sorbonne had no rooms in which they could work. At last they turned again to the School of Physics where Pierre taught. Here they found a shed. In the past, medical students had dissected cadavers in it. Now no one wanted it. It had an earthen floor, a leaky roof, and no ventilation. In summer it was steamy hot. In winter it was freezing cold. The Curies moved in.

Soon they were busy at work. Pierre, they decided, would

do experiments to get to know the properties of radium better. Marie would work at separating it from other elements. Her job was physically harder. She had to stir and pour and carry huge jars of liquid all day long, day after day.

Finally, after almost four years of back-breaking work in the miserable little shed, Marie had prepared one decigram (thirty-five ten-thousandths of an ounce) of pure radium. She calculated its atomic weight (225). Other scientists were convinced. Radium was now officially an element.

The Curies were extremely happy during this period of their life together, even though they were living in poverty. Scientists all over the world realized the great work they were doing. But the French government seemed blind to it, and did nothing to help them.

The Sorbonne offered no help either. In 1898 Pierre applied for a job there. It would have paid much more and he could have spent more time doing research and less time teaching. But he didn't get the job.

Nor was he elected to the Academy of Science, even though many other scientists thought he should be. Pierre, a scientist, was never very good at selling himself.

Then, in 1900, the University of Geneva in Switzerland offered jobs to both Pierre and Marie. Pierre would be making twenty times as much money as he earned at the School of Physics. He would have a laboratory with two assistants and all the equipment he needed. What a temptation!

At last, though, Pierre turned down the offer. To go to Geneva and prepare to teach new courses would interrupt the Curies' work on radium for months. He just couldn't do that. Neither could Marie.

Instead, Pierre took an extra job teaching at an annex of the Sorbonne. Marie found a job, too, teaching at a girls' high school. These extra jobs helped the family finances. But they did not help the Curies find a decent place in which to work.

In 1902, Professor Paul Appell, one of Marie's former teachers, wanted to nominate Pierre for the Legion of Honor, one of France's most distinguished awards. Pierre wouldn't let him. He didn't need a medal. He needed a laboratory.

Both he and Marie continued to assure their families and friends that they were in good health. But as the years passed and they worked so hard in that terrible shed, both became weak. Pierre had pains in his legs. The doctors called his problem "rheumatism," but they weren't really sure what was wrong. Marie grew thin and pale, both from overwork and from worrying about Pierre.

Then, in 1902, a chain of sad events began. First Marie's father died. She rushed back to Poland, but was too late to see him alive. She stood in front of his coffin and begged him to forgive her for moving to France.

Finally her brother and sisters convinced her that she

wasn't being fair to herself. The work she had done in France had meant a great deal to their father. He had been extremely proud of her. That was what she must remember.

But Marie could not shake her sadness or her tiredness. Once again her life seemed to be beset by cruel events. In the fall she began sleepwalking. The following summer she lost an unborn child. A little later, Bronya's son died. And, along with everything else, Marie kept worrying about Pierre.

The Curies didn't believe in feeling sorry for themselves or complaining. But just once during this difficult period, Pierre said, "It's pretty hard, this life that we have chosen."

His words frightened Marie.

"Pierre," she gasped, "If one of us disappeared, the other should not survive. We can't exist without each other, can we?"

But Pierre the scientist could not accept this.

"You are wrong," he said. "Whatever happens, even if one had to go on like a body without a soul, one must work just the same."

And work the Curies did. During the years from 1899 to 1904, they published thirty-two different papers. Scientists from around the world wrote to them about the discoveries and they wrote back. Meanwhile, they learned more and more about radium.

Working with other scientists, Pierre found out that the strange new element did wonderful things for sick people.

When used correctly, it killed diseased cells and helped cure growths, tumors, and even some kinds of cancer.

As soon as the world learned about this, radium became big business. A new industry was created; companies were formed for the sole purpose of extracting pure radium. Even the Academy of Science sat up and took notice. In 1902, they gave twenty thousand francs to the Curies to prepare more radium.

The Curies now had an important decision to make. They could patent their method of getting radium from pitchblende. That meant they would control the production of radium all over the world. They would become very rich people. Or they could share their knowledge freely with anyone who asked.

It was a simple choice and, for them, a simple decision. They could not keep their information to themselves. In Marie's words, "It is impossible. It would be contrary to the scientific spirit."

In the meantime, Marie found enough hours in 1903 to obtain a doctor's degree. She had been so busy working with radium that she had never gotten around to finishing her thesis about it. At last, though, she stood in the students' hall at the Sorbonne and answered the examiners' questions. Then the president of the Faculty of Science awarded the degree.

"The University of Paris accords you the title of doctor of

physical science," he said, "with the mention '*très honorable*' (very honorable). And in the name of the jury, madame, I wish to express to you all our congratulations."

They might sound like stuffy, formal words. But to those used to the ways of the Sorbonne, they were like cannons firing and skyrockets flaring. Marie's professors were very proud of her indeed.

Now that the world had heard about radium—and just a little about what it could do—people began to show more interest in the Curies themselves.

First the Royal Institution in England invited Pierre to lecture on radium. Then the Royal Society of London awarded the Davy Medal to both Marie and Pierre. Marie was ill at the time, so Pierre went to England to accept it.

He brought back a huge gold medal with their names on it. For some reason, the Curies couldn't find any place in their house to put it. So they gave it to six-year-old Irène to play with. She thought it made a splendid toy.

Near the end of 1903 came the greatest award of all. The Academy of Science in Stockholm decided to divide the Nobel Prize in physics for that year between Henri Becquerel and the Curies. The Nobel Prize—one of the world's highest honors! But Marie and Pierre couldn't go to Stockholm to collect it in person. Marie still didn't feel well and neither could leave their teaching duties long enough for the journey.

But they were able to enjoy the money that came with the prize. Pierre at last was able to quit his job at the School of Physics. They hired a laboratory assistant. They installed a modern bathroom in their home.

The Curies gave gifts, too—gifts to family members, to friends, to scientific groups. One of Marie's students at the high school needed financial help. Marie helped her. A Frenchwoman who had once taught Marie now lived in Poland and wanted to visit her homeland again. Marie paid for the trip.

It was wonderful to be able to do things for others at last. The Curies were grateful for the money the Nobel Prize brought them. But they were not grateful for the publicity.

Suddenly it seemed as if everyone in the world were writing to them, visiting them, talking to them, and taking their pictures. By nature, Marie and Pierre Curie were people who hated being in the public eye. When it began to keep them from doing their work, they became even more upset.

Marie wanted to work in her laboratory, not read a letter from some man who wanted to name a racehorse after her. And Pierre wrote to a friend: "I long for calmer days passed in a quiet place, where lectures will be forbidden and newspapermen persecuted."

Pierre's pains still bothered him and, in 1904, Marie was pregnant again. She was also exhausted. Bronya came from Poland to help at the child's birth. On December 6, 1904, the

Marie with her daughters, Irène (left) and Ève

Curies had another little daughter, whom they called Ève. Marie had to rest for a while after the birth and that proved to be just what she needed. When she went back to work, she felt much better.

Something else happened in 1905 to make Marie feel better. Some of the Russian people rebelled against the tsar and his government. The Polish people were elated. Maybe they, too, would be freed from Russian oppression. In the end, the 1905 revolution was not successful. But maybe in the future...

About this time the Curies actually broke down and bought some furniture. Now they could entertain small groups of friends in their home. Most of these friends were scientists, of course. But the Curies also got to know an American dancer, Loie Fuller, and the famous French sculptor Auguste Rodin.

It was also in 1905 that the Academy of Science finally came to its senses and made Pierre a member. That happened in July. In October, Pierre wrote to a friend, "I have not yet discovered what is the use of the Academy." Honors never would mean much to the Curies!

What did mean something, though, was the fact that the Sorbonne at last offered Pierre a professor's job. At least it meant something until he found out that the new appointment did not include a laboratory. No laboratory, no job, he told them.

It took a while, but at last arrangements for a laboratory were made. And Pierre was to have three assistants, one of whom was to be Marie. For the first time, she would be paid a salary for her work. Finally life seemed about to be a little kinder to the Curies.

Chapter 9

THE DARK YEARS

Thursday, April 19, 1906, was a gray, rainy day. Both Marie and Pierre had to go out. Marie did not get home again until six in the evening. When she stepped into the house, several old friends were waiting for her. It was her former professor, Paul Appell, who told her the terrible news.

Pierre was dead. He had stepped into the path of a horse-drawn wagon. The driver had not been able to stop the horses in time. One wheel of the wagon had crushed Pierre's skull. It had been an accident, a horrible accident. Onlookers had screamed. The driver of the wagon had wept. But it was too late. Pierre was dead.

"What was he dreaming of this time?" muttered old Dr. Curie again and again, with tears on his face.

A great grief makes some people angry. That is their way of handling pain. But Marie did not become angry. Nor did she weep. She stood there, cold as stone and utterly alone. Finally she asked that Pierre's body be brought home. She sent Irène to a neighbor. She wired her family in Warsaw. Then she sat down in the rain-soaked garden and stared into space. It wasn't until Pierre's brother Jacques arrived the next day that she was able to cry.

Even those tears did not last long. Mechanically, Marie made arrangements for the funeral. It could have been a huge public affair. But she would not allow that. No, Pierre would be buried in the tomb at Sceaux where his mother lay. And only his family and closest friends would take him there.

Of course, it was not possible to avoid newspaper reporters entirely. They hid behind tombstones at the cemetery and watched. Later one of them wrote that Marie had taken a bouquet of flowers and, one by one, torn the blossoms from their stems and scattered them on the coffin. But even as she did this, her eyes were dry and staring.

Weeks went by and still Marie did not talk to anyone about her dreadful sorrow.

She told little Irène what had happened and the child cried. But she was really still too young to understand. Baby Ève, of course, understood nothing.

Finally Marie found one person with whom she could share her feelings—Pierre. She began to keep a diary and in it she wrote long letters to him, spotted and blurred by tears.

"Everything is over," she wrote one day. "Pierre is sleeping his last sleep beneath the earth; it is the end of everything, everything, everything."

To her friends and family, it sometimes seemed as if Marie, too, had died. Dr. Curie, Jacques, Marie's brother Joseph, and her sister Bronya all gathered around her. They hoped to take care of her and plan for her future. At the moment she could not do those things for herself.

One decision Marie did make, though. The day of Pierre's funeral, the French government offered to give a pension to her and the children.

"I don't want a pension," Marie said firmly. "I am young enough to earn my living and that of my children." Might she have been thinking, too, of all the times the French government had ignored Pierre and his work when he was alive?

But how was she to earn that living? And who would carry on Pierre's work—both research and teaching—at the Sorbonne? To Jacques Curie and Pierre's close friend, Georges Gouy, the answer was obvious. Pierre's job must go to Marie.

Such a thing was unheard of in France. No woman had ever been a professor at the Sorbonne. But the authorities had to admit that Jacques and Georges were right. No one else could do the job. So on May 13, 1906, they offered it to Marie.

Her reply was simple. "I will try."

And still she wrote those long letters to Pierre. She told him about the job. She told him which flowers were in bloom. She told him about the children.

When summer came, she decided to stay in Paris to prepare the courses she would be teaching. Little Ève went on

79

vacation with Dr. Curie. Irène's Aunt Hela took her for a summer by the sea.

When everyone returned in the autumn, Dr. Curie asked Marie if she still wanted him to live with her. Perhaps he was too much trouble now and she would be happier if he lived elsewhere.

"If you went away it would hurt me," Marie told him. "But you should choose what you prefer."

Dr. Curie stayed.

On November 5, 1906, Marie was to give her first lecture at the Sorbonne. All Paris was buzzing about the great event. What would she say? What would she do? Would she talk about Pierre? The tiny lecture hall was packed with curious people.

Marie went first to the cemetery at Sceaux. There she talked to Pierre for a while. Then, at one-thirty, when her lecture was scheduled to begin, she walked into the hall. A roar of applause greeted her. She waited for it to end. Then she spoke.

"When one considers the progress that has been made in physics in the past ten years, one is surprised at the advance that has taken place in our ideas concerning electricity and matter. . . ."

The visitors must have looked a little puzzled. But many of the regular students began to cry. Marie had picked up Pierre's lectures exactly where he had left off.

Of course she could not devote all her time to her work at the Sorbonne. She had other responsibilities—Dr. Curie and the children. One of her first decisions was to find another house, away from the Boulevard Kellermann and all the memories that had gathered there. She found a house at 6 Rue du Chemin de Fer in Sceaux, not far from where Pierre was buried. She hired a Polish governess-housekeeper to help with the family. This woman, Marya Kamienska, was Joseph's sister-in-law and soon became a close friend.

Marie needed such friends. Her grief still haunted her and often she stared into space, her hands twitching. Sometimes she had terrible nightmares. Once she fainted in front of little Ève.

For a while, Dr. Curie's quiet strength did much to hold the family together. But in 1909 he became ill and had to stay in bed for a year. Marie tried to return to him all the loving care he had given to her and the children. In 1910 Dr. Curie died. Now Marie and her children were truly on their own.

She had spent a lot of time thinking about her daughters' education. Fresh air and exercise were important to her and she had taught them to enjoy sports at an early age. She didn't want them to spend long hours in stuffy schoolrooms. They could learn a great deal in a little time, she believed. When Irène was old enough to go to school, Marie set out to prove it.

A number of other professors who felt the same way joined her. They set up their own school, which was a little like the floating university in Poland had been. About ten children attended the school. One day they went to Professor Perrin's laboratory where he taught them chemistry. Another day they learned modeling from the sculptor Magrou. On Thursday afternoons Marie herself taught them physics.

This special school continued for two years, during which the children studied many subjects. None of them ever forgot the experiences. Some grew up to be scientists, including Irène Curie.

Meanwhile, Marie was deep in her own work again. She still taught at the girls' high school as well as at the Sorbonne. In 1908, she collected Pierre's writings and published them in book form as *The Works of Pierre Curie*. In 1910 she wrote a 971-page book about her own work, *Treatise on Radioactivity*.

She also had many students and assistants to supervise. An American philanthropist, Andrew Carnegie, gave money to offer scholarships to some of her students. One was especially dear to her, Jacques' son, Maurice Curie.

And then there was her research. No one had yet isolated radium as a pure metal. It had been isolated only as a salt. For months Marie struggled with complicated, tedious experiments. At last she succeeded. Marie looked with awe at the bright white solid. The procedures she had used in her experiment were so difficult that it has been done only one other time since then.

About this time, Marie also solved another radium problem. Because it existed in such tiny quantities, it was almost impossible to measure. Marie figured out a way of doing this by measuring the rays it emitted instead of measuring the radium itself.

After all the valuable work Marie had done with Pierre, the scientific world kept a close watch on her now. They knew they could expect more fine work in the future. She received many honorary doctorates from foreign schools. In 1910, France offered the Legion of Honor. But Marie remembered how Pierre had felt about that award. She followed his example and turned it down.

But, like Pierre, she did let herself be nominated for membership in the French Academy of Science. She had no idea what she was getting into, or she never would have agreed to the nomination. At once it set off a battle.

The scientists who wanted her in the academy pointed to the tremendous amount of work she had done. Other scientists disagreed. "She's a woman," they said. "We don't allow women in the academy." The arguments grew more and more nasty. Marie watched and listened, appalled.

Finally the vote was taken. Marie's assistants were certain of the outcome. They even bought a congratulatory bouquet of flowers for her. But they were wrong. Marie missed being elected by one or two votes. Quietly, one of the assistants got rid of the flowers. Marie herself said nothing. She just kept on working.

Once again the Swedish Academy of Science stepped in where the French academy had failed. In December of 1911, they honored her with the Nobel Prize in chemistry for that year. No one—no man or woman—had ever won two Nobel Prizes before.

This honor did mean something to Marie. And, even though she was ill at the time, she went to Stockholm to collect the prize. Bronya and young Irène went with her. The Swedes arranged special celebrations, and Marie was deeply grateful for their warm hospitality.

That hospitality probably meant even more to her because of another battle she was fighting at home. No person can accomplish great things without stirring up jealousy in the hearts of people who are not so gifted. Marie tried to ignore such jealousies, but they were still there, swirling around her.

It would have been difficult to attack her in the area of her work. The whole world knew of her accomplishments with radium. So some people decided to attack her personal life instead. They accused her of having a love affair with a young scientist, Paul Langevin. Langevin had been a friend of Pierre and was still her friend. This young man's own marriage was breaking up. The troublemakers saw no reason not to blame the breakup on Marie Curie.

People wrote articles for newspapers, expressing their opinions on the matter. Some extraordinarily silly men fought duels with guns or swords. And people with no minds of their own sent anonymous letters or stood outside her house, shouting and throwing stones.

Marie suffered terribly during this ordeal. Her real friends and her family rushed to be with her and protect her. That helped, but her health had reached its limits. On December 29, 1911, she was taken to a nursing home. No one expected her to live.

But Marie fought back. By the end of February, she was able to attend a scientific meeting. Then, in March, she had an operation on her kidneys that was supposed to improve her health.

The operation was successful, but it took Marie a long time to recover from it. She was pale and thin and could barely stand up by herself. Sometimes she ran a high fever. Sometimes she was in pain. For a time she tried to recuperate in France, but people there simply would not let her alone. So at last she took Irène and Ève and went to stay with a friend in England.

While she was still trying to get well, Marie had to make a heartbreaking decision. A group of Polish scientists wanted to build a laboratory for the study of radioactivity. And they wanted her to come back to Warsaw to be in charge of it.

How easy it would have been for her to go! She could have

left all the nasty battles behind. She could have spent the rest of her life in the land and with the people that she loved.

But Marie had never been one to run away from a battle. Besides, the French also were planning to build a radioactivity laboratory. That had been such an important part of the dream she and Pierre had shared. Could she turn her back on it now?

No, she decided, she couldn't. She refused the offer of the Polish scientists. But she did go to Warsaw in 1913 for the inauguration of the new laboratory. And what celebrations awaited her there! The Polish people truly did love and admire her.

One of them was a white-haired old woman named Miss Sikorska. Marie had attended her school when she was a small girl. Now the old woman sat and watched proudly as little Manya was honored by her country.

But what was this? Marie was leaving her place of honor and approaching the old woman. She was bending over her and kissing her on both cheeks. The rest of the audience burst into applause. And quiet little Miss Sikorska burst into tears.

Marie could not stay in Poland. Her work was elsewhere and she knew it. But coming home—even for a little while— made her very, very happy.

Chapter 10

RADIOLOGY AND WAR

By the summer of 1913, Marie felt much better. It was time to take her two girls and their governess on a vacation. This time, though, she chose a different kind of trip—a walking tour in the Swiss Alps.

The mountains were gorgeous, as she had known they would be. But perhaps the best part of the vacation was one of the other travelers—a scientist by the name of Albert Einstein. Now *there* was someone with whom Marie could talk. She knew just what he meant when he talked about the importance of finding answers to problems such as "transcendent relativity."

After this vacation, Marie had another project into which she threw all her energy. Some years back, French authorities had talked about building an Institute of Radium. But they got no further than talking. Then the Pasteur Institute took up the idea. *They* would build the laboratory Marie needed.

Shouts of outrage came from officials at the Sorbonne. Marie belonged to *them*, not to the Pasteur Institute. Finally both sides settled down and decided to build the institute together. There would be two parts. One would be for Marie's work in radioactivity. The other would be for biological research, especially methods of using radiology to cure sick people. Professor Claude Regaud would be in charge of this second part.

At last the building was under way. It would stand on a street in the grounds of the Sorbonne. That street had been renamed Rue Pierre Curie.

Marie had many ideas about the building's design. The laboratories must be big—huge—with large windows to let in as much light as possible. And there must be an elevator. Marie remembered what it was like to work in a dark shed and to stagger around with heavy jars of boiling liquid. She wasn't going to go through that again and neither would her co-workers.

But almost as important to her was the institute garden. She picked out the plane trees and lime trees herself and watched them being planted. The roses she planted herself. The beautiful things of nature seemed to mean even more as she grew older.

Finally, in July of 1914, the Institute of Radium was finished. Irène and Ève had already gone off to the French countryside with their governess for a vacation. Marie had some work to finish at the university, but would join them later. After vacation, she would be busy moving into the institute. And then, early in August, German armies marched into France. World War I had begun.

The Germans moved quickly—into Poland, across Belgium. Marie had no idea how her family back home in Poland were faring. But she was sure of one thing. She must play a part in this war.

Most of the men she knew had joined their military regiments. Many of the women became nurses. Marie could have become a nurse, too. But somehow that didn't seem the answer.

So she took a long, scientific look at the medical service and discovered what she thought was a terrible gap. Very few hospitals anywhere in France had X-ray equipment. The few places that did thought of it as a luxury.

A luxury? When X-rays could be used to help surgeons locate bullets and shrapnel? When countless wounded soldiers could be spared unnecessary suffering? Marie knew a good deal about X-rays, although she had never worked with them herself. There was no time like the present to begin. First she made a list of all the X-ray equipment available. She talked to manufacturers and obtained more. Then she had it given to hospitals around Paris.

Meanwhile, the Germans drew closer to the city. Marie's children were safe with their Uncle Jacques. She was quite certain that she'd be all right, too, even if the enemy did occupy the city. But there was the gram of radium at the laboratory. What if it fell into German hands?

Marie packed it into a special case and took a train for

Bordeaux. Crowds of other people were also fleeing from Paris to western France. But they didn't do what Marie did. She deposited her radium in a bank vault in Bordeaux. Then she took another train back to Paris.

Fortunately, the Germans didn't get as far as Paris. Before long, Marie was able to send for her daughters. It was time for Ève to return to school. Irène had decided to study for a nurse's diploma.

Marie herself still hadn't finished with X-ray equipment. It was all well and good to have such things at the hospitals. But they were needed somewhere else—at the battlefronts. And Marie knew how to get them there.

Suddenly all sorts of people found themselves being pestered by a determined little scientist. She told wealthy women that she needed their limousines. She told military officials that she wanted all the papers and permits she would need for her work.

It did no good to argue with her. Soon she had twenty cars. She took them to her laboratory and, one by one, transformed them. Into each she put an X-ray machine (called a Roentgen machine after the man who discovered X-rays in 1895). Into each also went a generator that could be driven by the car's engine and all the plates, screens, and other items necessary for taking X-rays.

At last the cars, now traveling X-ray units, were ready to head for whatever battlefield needed them. The soldiers called them "little Curies." They weren't Marie's only X-ray project. She also set up two hundred permanent X-ray units. Thanks to her, by the time the war ended, a million soldiers had had better treatment for their injuries because of X-rays.

Marie didn't sit safely at home while all this was going on. She kept one of the little Curies for herself. When a call came, she and a military chauffeur set off for wherever they were needed. Once there, she unloaded her equipment and the chauffeur started the motor. Within half an hour, she was ready for business.

Sometimes the surgeon operated right next to the X-ray machine. If a surgeon had to operate elsewhere, Marie would help by taking a photograph or drawing a picture of what the machine showed. A number of surgeons had never heard of X-rays. They thought Marie was crazy. But after they saw what the machine could do, they thought she had worked a miracle.

One day her chauffeur accidently flipped over Marie's little Curie in a ditch. Cases full of equipment crashed down on Marie, almost burying her. Surely all the radiological plates were broken. The thought of this made her furious. Then she heard an anxious little whisper.

"Madame! Madame! Are you dead?"

It was her chauffeur. Marie burst out laughing.

During the war, she traveled all over France in her little Curie. She even served at a number of Belgian hospitals.

Two of her co-workers at the Hoogstade hospital were King Albert and Queen Elizabeth of Belgium. But her favorite co-worker was her own daughter, Irène. Irène was seventeen now and old enough to help. So Marie gave her a quick course in radiology and sent her out on missions of her own.

War work took up much of the time Marie could have spent at her new institute. But time was not the only sacrifice she made for her adopted country. She gave the French government all the gold she possessed (including her scientific medals) and all the money she had won with her second Nobel Prize.

The government insisted that these gifts were only loans that would eventually be repaid. But Marie knew she would never see the money again. She was right. She did get the medals back, however. The officials said they couldn't possibly melt down such glorious things. Marie shrugged. She thought they were being gloriously foolish.

Meanwhile, there was still work to be done at the institute. First she had to pack all her equipment from the old laboratory and move it. Then she had to get the precious gram of radium back from Bordeaux. She could "milk" that radium each week for the gases it gave off. The gases were then sent in tubes to various hospitals where they were used to treat scars and other skin problems.

There were so many ways in which radiology could help in the war. But again and again Marie ran up against the same dilemma. There weren't enough people who knew how to work in this special field of science.

Finally she decided to offer a course in radiology at the institute. Twenty nurses signed up for the first course. By the end of the war, Marie had trained 150 technicians. Not all of them had started out as scientists or medical people. One woman was a chambermaid. But Marie Curie was a good teacher and so were her assistants—including Irène.

Other countries asked for her help with radiology, too. Belgium, Italy, and the United States all turned to her. Marie helped willingly.

Then came the long-awaited day when Germany was defeated and the war ended. Paris went mad with joy. Even quiet Marie got into her little Curie and drove through the streets with cheering friends perched on the roof of the battered old car.

For Marie there were two victories to celebrate. Not only had France won, but her beloved Poland was free at last.

"We have seen that resurrection of our country which has been our dream," she wrote to her brother Joseph. "Like you, I have faith in the future."

Chapter 11

JOURNEYS

Marie's own future did not look especially bright. The war had swallowed up all her savings and taken a terrible toll on her health. True, she had the salary from her teaching job at the Sorbonne. But for a while, she wasn't sure if she was strong enough to continue teaching.

Still, she kept going. In many ways Marie Curie was like her mother. She certainly followed the same rule: You did what had to be done. Before long she plunged back into her work at the institute and had written another book, *Radiology in War*.

The end of the war also gave her time to pay more attention to her daughters, who were now young women. Irène knew exactly what she wanted to do. She would be a scientist—a physicist—and carry on the work her father and mother had begun. Secretly, Marie hoped that Ève would become a doctor. But the young girl was less sure about what she wanted to do. She thought she might like a career in music.

Although they were so different, Marie loved both her daughters equally and tenderly. In 1919 she wrote to them: "You are in all truth a great fortune to me, and I hope life still holds for me a few good years of existence in common with you."

Some of the best times the three had together were at the little seaside village of Larcouëst in the part of France called Brittany. Three classes of people stayed in Larcouëst—peasants, sailors, and professors from the Sorbonne. The professors had to become sailors, too, or they were laughed out of the group. That was no problem for Marie and her daughters. They loved the water. Marie was an excellent swimmer and sometimes swam long distances out to sea.

She thought about those peaceful swims when she made another kind of journey by water. It all began with Mrs. William Brown Meloney, a tiny, gray-haired American woman. Mrs. Meloney was a New York magazine editor who had always admired Marie. For years she had wanted to meet the famous scientist. Finally, she did.

While they were talking, Mrs. Meloney asked Marie what one thing in the world she most wanted. Marie said a gram of radium to use for research. (The radium she already had was kept only for use in cancer treatment.)

At that time, a gram of radium cost $100,000. Mrs. Meloney was determined to get it. It would be a gift from the United States to Marie Curie.

Back home, she made an appeal to all women in the United States—rich and poor. Money poured in, sometimes as big checks, sometimes as coins or a few crumpled, hard-earned bills. Before a year had passed, Mrs. Meloney was able to write Marie: "The money has been found. The radium is yours."

But Mrs. Meloney had one request to make in return. She wanted Marie to visit the United States and collect the radium in person. Irène and Ève also were invited.

Marie was uneasy at the prospect of such a long trip and so many strangers. But she was touched and grateful for all that Mrs. Meloney had done. So she summoned her courage and, with Irène and Ève, climbed aboard the ship *Olympic*.

The sea journey itself was not much fun. Marie felt dizzy the entire time. But her enthusiastic welcome in the United States almost knocked her over. From city to city she traveled. Everywhere people greeted her with cheers, flowers, prizes, and other honors.

Marie was soon exhausted by all this activity. Twice she had to break her journey and rest. But she was happy, too. Honors did not mean much to her. But knowing that millions of Americans loved her and respected her work meant a very great deal.

On May 20, 1921, she visited the White House, where President Warren Harding gave to her a coffer containing "imitation radium." (The real radium was still safe at a factory, waiting for the trip back to France.) But Marie would never own such a valuable thing herself. Science must own it. So she made it a gift to her laboratory.

Many other journeys followed this trip to the United States. Earlier in her career, Marie might have avoided them. She really did prefer a quiet life, and her health gave her many problems. But she realized now that fame brought with it certain responsibilities. Sometimes her presence at the beginning of a new project guaranteed its success.

So off she went to such places as Italy, Holland, England, Czechoslovakia, Spain, and even Rio de Janeiro, Brazil. Some of her favorite souvenirs from the trips were sturdy menus from the banquets she had attended. She didn't keep them to recall what she had eaten. She liked to use the unprinted backs for mathematical calculations!

Marie didn't lose her interest in politics. Just after World War I, a family of countries called the League of Nations was formed. Marie believed passionately in the league. Its purpose was to promote peace and cooperation among the countries of the world. That was a purpose she wanted to work for.

In 1922, she was elected to the league's International Committee on Intellectual Cooperation. She happily accepted. This meant still more journeys.

There had to be better ways for scientists from different countries to work together, Marie believed. They should coordinate their publications. They should all use the same scientific terms and symbols. Scientists ought to be able to copyright their work. That way they could earn money from it and would not always have to fight poverty. And, most important of all, there should be international scientific scholarships for talented young people.

Marie also had a dream for Poland. Now that it was a free country, she wanted an Institute of Radium to be built in Warsaw. But that would take a great amount of money, which Poland didn't have.

Poland would get the money, Marie decided. The Polish people themselves would raise it by "buying bricks" for the institute.

Marie's sister Bronya also worked hard at the project, which went on for several years. Finally the buildings were completed. But one problem still remained. There was no radium.

So again Marie turned to her American friend, Mrs. Meloney, who at once accepted the challenge. In 1929, Marie again sailed to the United States to receive a gram of radium, this time from President Herbert Hoover. She made several journeys to Poland, too, as she worked on the project. In 1932, she was able to make a final trip for the inauguration of the Institute of Radium.

During those years after World War I, the French people decided it was time to pay tribute to Marie Curie. In 1922, the French Academy of Medicine elected her a member. This meant she was the first woman ever to join a French academy.

Marie Curie holding a 1934 conference at the Conservatory of
Arts and Techniques of Paris

In 1923, during a celebration of the twenty-fifth anniversary of the discovery of radium, the French government gave to Marie a pension of forty thousand francs a year in thanks for her work. Finally, after a lifetime of financial problems, she no longer had to worry about money.

Hela, Bronya, and Joseph came all the way from Poland for the celebration. One important person after another spoke—including the president of France.

Then, last of all, it was Marie's turn to speak. She thanked everyone for what they had done. She talked about Pierre, but she didn't mention herself. Instead, she begged everyone to support the Institute of Radium. So much valuable work still had to be done there!

Chapter 12

THE LAST YEARS

Marie was often tired now. She still insisted on working twelve to fourteen hours a day. Late in the evening when she finally came home from her laboratory to the apartment on the Île Saint-Louis, the three flights of stairs seemed very long.

A few changes had taken place in that apartment. It was rather bare, as all the Curie homes had been. It contained a cat. The Curies always had cats. But it also contained a grand piano—for Ève. And Irène was no longer there. In 1926, she had married a brilliant young scientist from the institute, Frédéric Joliot. Before long, the young couple gave Marie a granddaughter, Hélène.

Marie had a maid now, and a chauffeur. The pension from the government certainly had solved her financial problems. But she never was at ease spending money on herself. On the rare occasions when she did buy a new dress, she always picked the least expensive one in the shop.

There were two things, though, on which she did enjoy spending money. One was houses. She built a house at Larcouëst and another in the south of France. She would have liked to leave the Île Saint-Louis apartment and build still another house at Sceaux. But somehow there never seemed to be enough time to get all that done.

Marie also enjoyed spending money on plants. Wherever she went—to one of her houses or to the institute—she planted things. It was as if the beauty of growing things outside made up for the bareness inside her homes and laboratory.

Some changes had taken place at the institute, too. Marie no longer spent as much time on her own research. Instead, she taught and supervised assistants and students from all over the world. When she was younger, their interruptions would have driven her mad. But now she realized that working with them was the best thing she could do for science. They would be the ones to continue her work when she was gone.

When she wasn't teaching, she was out demanding support for her institute. She never asked for much for herself. But when it came to the institute, she was like a mother tiger protecting her cub. Radium, scholarships, grants, equipment—she wanted them all. And she got them.

She also used up great quantities of paper and ink. Between 1919 and 1934, scientists at the institute published 483 papers. Thirty-one of these were written by Marie.

Then there were all the letters that needed to be answered. She never answered fan letters. But she responded to all the questions scientists wrote to ask her.

As the years passed, a new problem emerged to make her life and her work more difficult. Marie began to have trouble with her eyes. For a while it seemed as if cataracts would leave her blind. Finally, she had a series of operations. They helped, but it was a long time before she could see well enough again to make careful measurements in her laboratory.

Meanwhile, she didn't want anyone except her family to know what was wrong. She even used a false name when she had her operations. Her students and assistants at the institute must have realized what was happening. But they never let her know that they knew.

Another enemy was also eating away at Marie's health. For thirty-five years she had worked with radium and other radioactive materials. At that time, no one knew how dangerous years of exposure to radioactive rays could be. Marie had burns on her hands, but to her they were just a little annoyance that went with the job.

As time went by, and scientists learned more, they began to be more careful when working with radioactive substances. Marie became very strict with her workers at the institute. They had to use tongs and lead shields instead of touching the tubes containing the substances. They had to have regular blood tests to make certain they weren't contaminated by the rays.

Marie had a blood test that showed her blood was abnormal. That seemed not to bother her any more than the burns on her hands. She had no idea that the radiation attacking her blood was probably also responsible for all the pains and bouts of ill health that had plagued both her and Pierre throughout the years.

What did bother her was the news that she had a gallstone. Marie didn't want any more operations. She tried to prove to herself and everyone else that she was perfectly healthy. She took part in various sports and went on trips. She was fine, just fine.

But on one of those trips, a long one into the country with Bronya, she caught a cold or the flu. And from then on, she was never able to get rid of a slight fever.

Time passed and the fever grew worse. Sometimes she felt as if she were burning up. At other times she shook with chills.

"You must stay in bed," a doctor told her. For as long as possible, Marie ignored this advice. She went to her laboratory almost every day and worked as long as she could.

But one day in May of 1934, she felt especially ill. Perhaps she would go home early. Gently she touched her beloved "physics apparatus." Then she went into the garden. One of the rose plants was not doing well. She asked a worker to take care of it. After that she left the institute. She would never return.

Her doctors weren't quite sure what was wrong with her.

Test after test was run. Finally someone suggested that she must go to a sanatarium in the mountains. Marie agreed.

By the time she got there, her temperature was very high, over 104 degrees Fahrenheit. A specialist looked at her blood tests. She had pernicious anemia, he said. He promised there would be no operation. None could have helped. She was dying. Doctors would later name her disease leukemia, caused by overexposure to radiation.

Strangely enough, Marie, the scientist, did not realize how ill she was. She thought she would be well enough to go back to work in the autumn. She looked forward to building the house at Sceaux. She was fairly certain that Irène and Frédéric would win the Nobel Prize in a few months for their work in atomic research. (She was right.)

No one took Marie's hope away from her. But finally her mind became confused. People faded away and only the work remained. One day she looked at a teacup and asked, "Was it done with radium or with mesothorium?"

A doctor came to give her an injection while she lay in bed.

"I don't want it," she said. "I want to be let alone." Those were her last words.

At dawn on July 4, 1934, Marie died. A doctor held one of her hands. Her daughter Ève held the other.

On July 6, she was buried with Pierre and his parents in the cemetery at Sceaux. It was a small funeral with only family, friends, and co-workers to say good-bye to her. No

This is one of the last photos of Marie Curie, taken shortly before her death on July 4, 1934.

one made any speeches. But into her open grave Joseph and Bronya each threw a handful of earth brought from Poland.

A year after her death, Marie's last book was published. It was called, simply, *Radioactivity*. Marie Curie had dedicated herself to radioactivity. It had taken her life. But because of her, it also gave—and still gives—life to countless people.

Marie Curie 1867-1934

1867 A Swede, Alfred Nobel, patents dynamite. Karl Marx publishes Volume I of *Das Kapital*. In the United States, three Reconstruction Acts passed; U.S. buys Alaska from Russia. In Mexico, Emperor Maximilian executed. Military rule abolished in Japan.

1868 Revolution in Spain; Queen Isabella II deposed. United States President Andrew Johnson impeached by House, acquitted by Senate; Ulysses S. Grant elected president.

1869 World's first transcontinental railroad completed in United States. Suez Canal opens.

1870 Beginning of Franco-Prussian War. Revolution in France.

1871 Treaty of Frankfurt ends Franco-Prussian War. William Marcy (Boss) Tweed indicted for fraud in New York City. Feudalism banned in Japan.

1874 Disraeli becomes British prime minister, second time. In the United States, National Woman's Christian Temperance Union formed.

1876 Queen Victoria of England proclaimed Empress of India. Battle of Little Bighorn in the United States; General Custer defeated by Sioux and Cheyenne; Alexander Graham Bell patents telephone. Famine in India.

1877 In the United States, Reconstruction ends in the South. Porfirio Díaz becomes president of Mexico. Rebellion in Japan put down.

1878 In the United States, Albert A. Michelson accurately measures speed of light at 186,508 miles per second. Edison patents phonograph.

1879 Edison invents first practical electric light. Afghans cede Khyber Pass, among other territories, to British.

1880 Boers revolt against British in Transvaal.

1881 Pasteur vaccinates sheep against anthrax. Alexander II of Russia assassinated. In the United States, President Garfield assassinated. In South Africa, British suffer defeat by Boers; grant self-rule to Transvaal.

1883 Program of social reform begun in Germany. Discovery by Edison that electric current can be sent through space.

1884 South West Africa becomes German protectorate. British try to strengthen position in South Africa.

1885 Pasteur develops rabies vaccination. In the United States, Apache Indians renew war with whites. Spain, Germany, and Britain claim new protectorates in Africa. Russian-Afghan border dispute.

1887 Queen Victoria of England celebrates Golden Jubilee. United States obtains right to build naval base at Pearl Harbor, Hawaii. French form Indo-China.

1889 Rebellion in Crete smashed by Turks. In the United States, first whites settle in Oklahoma; several states pass first antitrust laws. In Africa, Cecil Rhodes of Britain gains control of territory north of Transvaal and west of Mozambique. New Japanese constitution.

1890 Bismarck dismissed as chancellor of Germany. In the United States, Sherman Antitrust Act passed; Battle of Wounded Knee; Sioux massacred. First general election in Japan.

1891 Triple Alliance renewed by Germany, Austria-Hungary, and Italy. Circuit Court of Appeals created by United States Congress.

1892 Panama Canal scandal in France. Famine in Russia. Nationalist movement gains momentum in India.

1893 France and Russia form alliance. In Austria, Sigmund Freud and Josef Breuer publish theories on psychoanalysis. In the United States, economic depression begins. New Zealand begins women's suffrage.

1894 French army officer Alfred Dreyfus falsely convicted of treason. Nicholas II, last tsar of Russia, takes throne. Pullman Company strike in Chicago led by Eugene V. Debs, who is jailed. In Africa, Uganda becomes protectorate of Britain; Dahomey becomes French protectorate. Korea and Japan go to war with China.

1895 Marie Sklodowska marries Pierre Curie. Guglielmo Marconi invents wireless telegraph. Cubans revolt against Spanish rule. Italians defeated in Ethiopia. Sino-Japanese War ended by Treaty of Shimonoseki.

1896 Cretans rebel against Turks. Frenchman Henri Becquerel discovers that uranium emits rays. In the United States, *Plessy* v. *Ferguson* Supreme Court decision makes "separate but equal" accommodations for blacks and whites legal.

1897 Crete becomes independent.

1898 Marie Curie coins the term *radioactivity*; discovers polonium and radium. Social Democratic party established in Russia. Spanish-American War; Treaty of Paris ending war results in the United States receiving Puerto Rico, Guam, and the Philippines. Cuba gains independence.

1899 Filipinos revolt against U.S. Wake Island annexed to U.S. Beginning of Boer War between British and Boers. Anglo-Egyptian government formed in the Sudan.

1900 Neils Bohr of Denmark proposes still-valid theory of how atom is structured. King of Italy assassinated. Hawaii becomes a U.S. territory. British win battles in the Boer War. Europeans continue to stake claims and define borders in Africa. Boxer Rebellion in China.

1901 German chemist Wilhelm Roentgen receives first Nobel Prize in physics for discovery of X-rays. Queen Victoria of England dies. In Russia, Social Revolutionary party is founded. United States President McKinley assassinated. Australia becomes a commonwealth.

1902 Marie and Pierre Curie discover properties of radium. Dutch physicists Pieter Zeeman and Hendrik Lorenz receive Nobel Prize in physics for their discovery of the effect of magnetism on radiation. Permanent Census Bureau established in the United States; Congress authorizes funds to build Panama Canal. Treaty of Vereeniging ends Boer War in Africa.

1903 Marie and Pierre Curie win Nobel Prize in physics for discovery of radioactive phenomenon. Menshevik and Bolshevik factions of the Russian Social Democratic party are born. United States recognizes Panama's independence from Colombia. United States and Panama sign Hay-Bunay-Varilla Treaty giving the U.S. the land across which the Panama Canal will be built. Orville and Wilbur Wright make first successful airplane flight.

1905 Nicholas II of Russia signs October Manifesto promising government reforms. German physicist Albert Einstein puts forth special theory of relativity. Russo-Japanese War (1904-05) ended by Treaty of Portsmouth. In China, Revolutionary League established by Sun Yat-sen.

1906 Pierre Curie dies. Marie Curie becomes first woman professor at Sorbonne, taking her husband's appointment. Dreyfus cleared of earlier charges and given Legion of Honor in France. President Theodore Roosevelt receives Nobel Peace Prize for his role in establishing peace conference that ended Russo-Japanese War. Sinai Peninsula becomes part of Egypt. Revolt in Cuba; Roosevelt sends in troops to restore peace.

1907 In the United States, the stock market falls; first Mother's Day. Sir Frederick Hopkins discovers importance of vitamins. In Africa, Transvaal and Orange Free State become self-governing.

1908 Revolution of the Young Turks in the Turkish Empire. Model-T car introduced. Canberra becomes capital of Australia.

1909 National Association for the Advancement of Colored People founded in the United States. Robert Peary reaches the North Pole.

1910 George V becomes king of England. Marie Curie's *Treatise on Radioactivity* published. In the United States, first Father's Day. British create Union of South Africa.

1911 Marie Curie wins Nobel Prize in chemistry for discovery of polonium and radium. Scottish physicist Charles Wilson invents the "cloud chamber," a device for studying atomic particles. Revolution in Mexico. United States sends troops to Mexican border to protect Americans. Republic of China established; Sun Yat-sen becomes president. Delhi becomes capital of India.

1912 Bill for home rule in Ireland introduced in parliament. United States Public Health Service founded. U.S. troops go to Cuba to protect U.S. interests there. U.S. troops also sent to Nicaragua during a rebellion to protect U.S. lives and interests there. Yüan Shih-kai takes control of Chinese government; Sun Yat-sen resigns.

1913 Serbians and Rumanians push for separation from Austro-Hungarian Empire. Income tax becomes federal law with passage of 16th Amendment to the U.S. Constitution; direct election of U.S. senators provided for in 17th Amendment. South Africa passes law restricting immigration of Asians.

1914 Serbian nationalist assassinates Austrian Archduke Francis Ferdinand at Sarajevo. Beginning of World War I between Allies (Britain, France, Russia, Belgium, and Serbia) and Central Powers (Austria-Hungary and Germany). All of Nigeria combined into one British colony and protectorate. Japan declares war on Germany.

1915 World War I continues. German zeppelins and submarines menace Britain. Tsar Nicholas II personally takes over command of Russian army. Japan tries to make China its protectorate. Sinking of ship *Lusitania* by Germans causes U.S. President Wilson to register protest. German colony of South West Africa conquered by South Africans.

1916 World War I continues. Paul von Hindenburg commands the German armies. British use tanks for first time on the western front at Battle of Somme. Francis P. Rouse develops a way to store blood. United States threatens to break off relations with Germany if it continues to attack unarmed ships. Belgians and Germans fight each other in Africa. China recognizes claims of Japan in southern Manchuria and Inner Mongolia.

1917 World War I continues. German use of submarines becomes more pervasive. Rebellion in French army follows heavy losses. China declares war on Germany and Austria. Revolution in Russia; Tsar Nicholas II abdicates; moderates take over the government; second Bolshevik revolution overthrows moderates. Armistice signed between Russia and Germany on eastern front. United States declares war on Germany; General Pershing heads U.S. troops in France; Selective Service Act passed; all men must register for the draft. Mexico adopts new constitution. Led by "Lawrence of Arabia" (Thomas Edward Lawrence), Arabs revolt against Turkish authorities; British defeat Turks at Baghdad. British give approval for formation of a Jewish state in Palestine (Balfour Declaration).

1918 Russia and Central Powers sign Treaty of Brest-Litovsk. Central Powers surrender to Allies. Civil war in Russia; royal family executed. U.S. President Wilson attends Paris Peace Conference; Supreme Court rules that the draft is constitutional; United States divided into four time zones; biochemist Herbert M. Evans discovers human beings have 48 chromosomes.

1919 Treaty of Versailles signed by Germany and Allies. Austria, Hungary, Bulgaria, and Turkey sign other peace treaties. World War I officially over. President Wilson designs League of Nations at Paris Peace Conference. U.S. does not join. 18th Amendment to U.S. Constitution, establishing prohibition, becomes law.

1920 Separate parliaments established for northern and southern Ireland. German Workers' party becomes Nationalist Socialist German Workers', or Nazi, party. U.S. women get the vote; President Wilson receives Nobel Peace Prize; first commercial radio broadcast originates in Pittsburgh at station KDKA. Civil war in China; no central government.

1921 At a conference in Paris, German reparations for war damages set at approximately $33 billion. Widespread famine in Russia. Economic depression in United States; insulin discovered by Canadian Frederick Banting and American Charles Best.

1922 Mussolini becomes dictator in Italy. Financial crisis in Germany. In United States, beginning of Teapot Dome scandal centering around illegal leasing of government oil reserves. Egypt becomes independent of Britain. Gandhi protests British rule in India; is imprisoned.

1923 Adolf Hitler imprisoned after unsuccessful attempt to take over German government; writes *Mein Kampf* in prison. U.S. President Harding dies suddenly; Calvin Coolidge becomes president. Rhodesia (Zimbabwe), a British colony in Africa, is granted its own government.

1924 Lenin dies in Russia; power struggle begins. Greece becomes a republic. U.S. Secretary of the Interior Albert B. Fall implicated in Teapot Dome scandal, is found guilty and later sent to prison.

1925 Paul von Hindenburg becomes president of Germany. In Wyoming, Nellie Tayloe Ross becomes first woman governor in United States. In Iran, the Pahlavi dynasty, which would last until 1979, is founded.

1927 Stalin gains control of government in Russia; Trotsky and followers exiled to provinces. Hindenburg rejects Germany's responsibility for starting World War I. First talking motion pictures are seen in U.S. movie theaters. U.S. Marines go to Nicaragua to protect U.S. interests during civil war. Chiang Kai-shek, Chinese Nationalist leader, takes control of Nanking and in 1928 it becomes capital of his new government.

1929 Alexander I, king of Yugoslavia, becomes dictator. In Germany, Heinrich Himmler becomes head of Nazi party S.S. In the United States, stock market crashes and Great Depression begins. In Mexico, the National Revolutionary party is founded. Arabs attack Jews in dispute over use of Wailing Wall in Jerusalem.

1930 Nazi party becomes dominant in German politics. Worldwide economic depression. U.S. Congress allots funds for public works projects and drought relief; Veterans Administration founded; Vannevar Bush pioneers the computer. Emperor Haile Selassie begins reign in Ethiopia. Gandhi leads protest against salt tax imposed in India by British authorities.

1931 British Commonwealth of Nations established. In Spain, government of Alfonso XIII topples. In New York City, Mayor James Walker is accused of political corruption. Egypt and Iraq sign treaty of friendship. Japanese invade Manchuria.

1932 Hitler continues to increase power in German parliament. Antonio de Oliveira Salazar begins 36-year dictatorship in Portugal. Franklin Delano Roosevelt becomes president of the United States; unemployment insurance established in Wisconsin; beginning of the "New Deal." Japanese invade China, seize Manchuria.

1933 Nazis burn German parliament building; Hitler establishes dictatorship. Spanish government puts down anarchists' rebellion. In the United States, national bank holiday; first "fireside chat"; a host of new federal programs designed to combat the depression.

1934 Hitler takes the title Führer (leader). Gaston Doumerque becomes French premier after financial scandal; restores faith in government. Nazis try to take over Austrian government. King Alexander I of Yugoslavia assassinated by Croatian terrorist. Lázaro Cárdenas becomes president of Mexico. Italians and Ethiopians fight over land in eastern Africa. Mao Tse-tung and Chinese Communists attacked by Chiang Kai-shek. Mao's followers travel with him across 6,000 miles of China on what is known as the "Long March." Marie Curie dies.

INDEX- *Page numbers in boldface type indicate illustrations.*

ABOUT THE AUTHOR

Carol Greene has a B.A. in English Literature from Park College, Parkville, Missouri and an M.A. in Musicology from Indiana University, Bloomington. She's worked with international exchange programs, taught music and writing, and edited children's books. She now works as a free-lance writer in St. Louis, Missouri and has had published over 20 books for children and a few for adults. When she isn't writing, Ms. Greene likes to read, travel, sing, and do volunteer work at her church. Her other books for Childrens Press include: *Enchantment of the World: England*; *The Super Snoops and the Missing Sleepers*; *Sandra Day O'Connor: First Woman on the Supreme Court*; *Rain! Rain!*; *Please, Wind?*; *Snow Joe*; and *The New True Book of Holidays Around the World*.